der

Dr. Orna Markus Den Zvi

Producer & International Distributor
eBookPro Publishing
www.ebook-pro.com

**The Personal Leader: Live with Purpose and Achieve Your Goals**
**Orna Markus Ben Zvi**

Translation: Lola Kreizman

Contact: Orna.positive@gmail.com
ISBN 9798787689907

# THE
# PERSONAL
# LEADER

## LIVE WITH PURPOSE AND ACHIEVE YOUR GOALS

DR. ORNA MARKUS BEN ZVI

# CONTENTS

# INTRODUCTION

My book is one of the hundreds of books that are published around the world each year, with the goal of helping people experience a life of emotional well-being, empowerment and success. And yet, I have the deep sense that many people, in Israel and around the world, will connect with the contents of my book, which was written in a style suitable for everyone.

This book, which for me is like a small child coming into the world, was not created in an instant. It is the fruit of writing and workshops that I led over the past twenty years in different institutions, in workshops for students, and in empowerment workshops for seniors and education faculties. It deals with the heart of the matter of topics that are on all of our minds: How we can live life powerfully, with inner peace and joy, and all this in the complex and challenging reality of the 21st century.

It is not my intention, and I do not for a moment presume to be a role model or inspiration. I aspire to share with you the insights I've had in different stages of my life, so they might help, even in the slightest, people who are dealing daily with the difficulties and challenges that life throws at us and which sometimes seem impossible to overcome. The ideas in the book have been formulating in my mind and consciousness over many years, during which I and those around me, experienced deep emotional processes.

I'll start at the beginning. Who am I?

My name is Dr. Orna Markus Ben-Zvi, and I am currently a retiree of the education system. I am in my sixties. I was born in Tel-Aviv, and when I first started out, I served as an adjutant officer in the IDF and finished with the rank of Captain after seven years of service.

I spent two years in Nigeria with my family who was there on business, then went on to finish my first degree and began working in the education system. After getting my Ph.D. in Gender Studies and Jewish History, I began work in the training department of the Ministry of Education, first, as a history instructor, and then later, as a national instructor for education and gender. I served in these roles for seven years, until my retirement.

During my many years as a teacher, homeroom teacher and other various roles I had in the high school where I taught, and during my studies for my Master's degree and then PhD, I faced one main challenge: How to combine a full-time teaching job (with all its many requirements aside from teaching: checking exams, preparing homework for the class, connecting with my students and their parents) with research and writing that demanded persistence, collecting material, concentration and scientific writing. And this on top of my duties as wife, mother, and later—grandmother. For this I required emotional strength, vitality and an inner wellspring from which I could draw encouragement and optimism in order to keep going and not be discouraged along the way.

In order to cheer up and not give up, and successfully withstand the professional challenges I faced while remaining emotionally balanced and happy, I used to write insights that came to me and empowering thoughts. For many years, these materials remained in a drawer and didn't see the light of day. I turned them into lectures, activities, workshops and presentations, which I delivered in various forums, and I even included these empowering messages in the education and gender workshops for education faculties. The participants of these different meetings reported that this content contributed to their emotional well-being, encouraged them to share their authentic voices, strengthened their sense of capability and urged them to create the reality they sought for themselves.

The contents of this book are organized by foundational topics, and I hope that reading this book will help people—both men and women—psychologically, spiritually, emotionally and practically, in dealing with the complex and challenging reality that every one of us faces throughout the course of our lives.

**Following the realization that these materials can be helpful to others, I decided to publish this book. I see it as a calling and a mission that I took upon myself.**

## SECTION 1

LEADERSHIP, MEANING AND RESPONSIBILITY
FOR OUR LIVES

# CHAPTER 1

# First and Foremost, Personal Leadership

**Personal leadership is taking personal responsibility for one's fate, course of life and consciousness.**

Many people believe that there is some external force arranging their lives for them. However, this belief—in destiny or in an external power that will come and save a person—blocks them. It doesn't allow them to act to advance themselves and their goals. They must know: salvation will always come from man himself—to himself.

Martin Luther King, leader of the civil rights movement for blacks in The United States, said: "If you can't fly then run, if you can't run then walk, if you can't walk then crawl, but whatever you do, you have to keep moving forward." (from his speech "What is your life's blueprint?" for Barratt junior high school students in Philadelphia, 1967.)

One of the main ideas of the Age of Enlightenment, which developed in Europe in the 18th century, states that every person is responsible for shaping their fate, and the same goes for the nations of the world. This is a rational attitude towards life, which places full responsibility on man for his fate and life. And indeed, the keys to our lives are in our hands and not in the hands of others, the hands of God, or the hands of fate or any other external force, real or imagined. Even people who experienced the most difficult situations imaginable, like in the Holocaust, testify that despite living in those horrifying times, they still had the free will to choose how to deal with the terrible and impossible events they experienced.

Venus Williams, the former world champion American tennis player, said in one of her speeches: "I don't focus on what I'm up against. I focus on my goals and I try to ignore the rest."

There are people living in constant passivity. They allow life to drag them on while they only react to the actions of other people or to circumstances that were forced upon them. They gave up their free will from the get-go. Other people sense that they are victims of life's circumstances, and they will feel frustration their whole lives that will affect their physical and mental health. Their passivity will weigh on them and their surroundings as well, and they will remain stuck and frozen in their life situation and won't initiate change or take steps to improve their reality. Passivity keeps a person stuck and, in fact, pulls them backward.

How does personal leadership manifest in our lives?

- **Personal leadership** is, first of all, setting goals. We will set for ourselves personal, professional and social ("lighthouse") goals and destinations, and imagine ourselves as far out and as wild as possible. Because every action begins with a dream.

- **Personal leadership** means that we are the ones who determine our daily routine:

We recognize emotional and other types of manipulations that certain people place on us, and do not let anyone manage us, not directly and not indirectly.

Leonardo Da Vinci, one of the great Renaissance artists, said: "It had long since come to my attention that people of accomplishment rarely sat back and let things happen to them. They went out and happened to things."

- **Personal leadership** allows us to navigate life through the entanglement of personal agendas, emotions and people, which include also complicated and unclear situations. It means taking responsibility for our connection and relationships with others, and also for the decision to lead and not be led.

- **Personal leadership** means that we will never be in the position of the victim. We will live a moral life that will include receiving and giving, and this giving and abundance will come back to us, because life has an internal truth of balance.

- **Personal leadership** demands that we try and understand the other, listen to them and know that we are thinking solely from our own (subjective) point of view. And we will always remember, that humanity will never be selective. It will treat and affect everyone.

- **Personal leadership** means that we will never need to use physical or verbal violence. We will know that we are part of the universe, part of the cosmic circle of life, and that the laws of nature apply to us. Our days are numbered, and so we must live life to the fullest and with the highest intensity.

- **Personal leadership** gives us the option of seeing beyond momentary distress. Thanks to it, we understand that failures and disappointments are a necessary part of the road to growth and improvement in all areas.

- **Personal leadership** is the realization that all solutions lay within us and that we do not need others in order to find the recipe for happiness. We must take responsibility for our happiness and for recharging our emotional batteries, and we must identify the tools and methods we will use to do this.

- **Personal leadership** is setting our own goals and heights, and not those that were set by social orders and norms. We must realize our own uniqueness and not be afraid to be extraordinary.

- **Personal leadership** determines that we must place boundaries for ourselves and for others and be assertive with them about our needs and desires.

- **Personal leadership** releases us from fears and anxieties that hold us back and allows for us to observe life from the perspective of fullness and not of lack. Thanks to it, we will be grateful for and appreciative of the gifts of life and give up suffering.

- **Personal leadership** is taking responsibility for our joy and conduct in life, and most importantly—it is the realization that almost everything is up to us, our consciousness, our persistence and willpower.

Abraham Lincoln, the 16th president of the United States, embodies in his life the definition of personal leadership. Lincoln was born in a rural and poor area, to a family with modest means and learned in school for merely one year. At age nine, he lost his mother, and since then, he began assisting his father with all his laborious farm work, which toughened his personality. He excelled at having a thirst for knowledge and education, studied on his own and became a lawyer. Lincoln experienced many losses on his political journey, and even suffered from depression. However, the great difficulties in his life strengthened his spirit. He was excellent in his reasonable and rational approach, and was known for his calmness and love for mankind. The nickname "honest Abe," which was given to him, expresses the admiration he received from the people of his time. Lincoln is considered to be one of the figures who had the greatest influences on the history of the United States. He strengthened the Union of the United States and prevented it from splitting following the Civil War, and he is responsible for abolishing slavery.

Barack Obama, the first black president of the United States, said: "Change will not come if we wait for some other person, or some other time. We are the ones we've been waiting for. We are the change that we seek." (From a speech he delivered on February 2nd, 2008, to his supporters, as provided by the Federal News Service and quoted in the New York Times).

\*\*\*

James Dean, the American film actor who became a cultural icon, said: "I can't change the direction of the wind, but I can adjust my sails to always reach my destination."

I wish for you all to always adjust your sails in your desired direction, so you may reach the destination you choose.

# CHAPTER 2

# Within Each of Us is an Inner Engine

**Within each one of us is an inner engine which carries us wherever we choose to go. Almost everything in life depends on us, on an inner decision, on our persistence and our willpower.**

In order to turn our lives into fulfilling, meaningful and happy ones, we need to believe that we have the ability to reach our goals, whatever they may be. We must be driven with the feeling of success and faith so that we can handle the challenges that we are faced with.

The feeling of personal capability is more important than the capability itself. In many people, there is great untapped potential that is not being realized, and they experience ongoing frustration in their lives. They haven't fulfilled their hidden potential because they do not believe in themselves and their abilities, nor do they have the emotional energy to deal with the difficulties along the way. Contrary to them, there are people who were not blessed with the most optimal natural abilities, and in spite of this, they will reach high professional and personal achievements. They will reach these heights thanks to their feelings of capability, thanks to the effort they will invest, thanks to the determination and optimism that enables them to deal with failures and keep moving forward. In the end it is the human spirit that is victorious and not their skills.

The singer Susan Boyle was determined to fulfill her dream of becoming a singer. She was born the youngest in a family of six sisters and four brothers. As a child, she was diagnosed with a learning disability and later on was diagnosed with Asperger Syndrome. In 2009, she performed on the most prominent talent show in all of Great Britain. At first, her physical appearance and older age generated some disrespect and raised some eyebrows among the viewers, but the moment she began singing, silence was cast in the hall and her wonderful voice penetrated everyone's hearts. Even the words of the song were symbolic: They were all about how there is no right time to fulfill a dream, no right age or right place. At any given moment, a person can decide to fulfill their aspirations with the help of strong faith and persistence, and so move forward toward their goal. Within merely a few days, the video of the performance gained forty-five million views, and Boyle became one of the most successful singers in Britain and the whole world.

It's true, we cannot be responsible for events that are out of our control, but our reaction to these events is in our own hands. In other words: The keys are inside. A positive attitude about life, the challenges it throws at us, the difficulties, and its various situations – will advance us in life, help us to be happier, more active, and to contribute to ourselves and to others, to family, to community and to society.

Too many people give up in advance on their dreams when they weigh their dream against the objective conditions, ones which they see as impossible obstacles. In this lies their biggest mistake. The cold and rational facts are lying. They do not take into consideration human passion, determination and willpower, which overcome, in many cases, all obstacles. See, for example, the beginning of the Zionist movement. In those days, its leaders, with Herzl at the head, were considered no more than dreamers, but were it not for their fantasy, we wouldn't be among the family of nations today and the State of Israel would not have been established.

Grace Hopper, an American pioneer in computer sciences, who was ground-breaking both in regard to her profession and in regard to gender, said: "A ship in harbor is safe—but that is not what ships were built for."

Helen Keller, the author and social activist who was deaf, blind and mute and became a worldwide inspiration, said: "Although the world is full of suffering, it is also full of the overcoming of it."

And yet, the entrepreneur Bill Gates, founder of Microsoft, said: "It's fine to celebrate success, but it is more important to heed the lessons of failure."

The conclusion: If we lose the magical, childish and innocent human ability—something to dream about, we lose the whole point of life. If so, let us turn the obstacle into a challenge: let us skip over the surrounding conditions that are blocking us and decide that from now on they are no longer relevant.

Let us remember: The key to the door of "the locked room" (a metaphor for those "dead ends" and "no-way-to-move-forward" feelings in life) is in our hands. It is in those very situations where we are feeling stuck in life—that we have the opportunity to go down a new path, fulfill our dreams and improve the quality of our lives.

So how do we move forward?

1. We **declare** the dream or challenge, write it down, and break down the overall mission into smaller tasks and sub-stages. This way, in a simple and practical way, the scary goal, which is perceived by us as too much to handle and unattainable, will suddenly become realistic and much less intimidating. Yes, yes, also Rome wasn't built in a day.
2. We **divide** the overall mission into goals and sub-stages, preferably with dates, and then start the journey. Before heading out, we'll equip ourselves with determination, faith and optimism.
3. We **remember** that the journey toward our goal will usually not be a short one. In a real and right process, there are no shortcuts but deep digging, furrow after furrow, and sometimes your metaphorical plow will encounter obstacles. When plowing a field, there will always be stumbling blocks in the way, this is the natural process.

"You don't have to see the whole staircase," said Martin Luther King, leader of the black civil rights movement in the United States, "just take the first step…"

✳✳✳

Remember! You—and only you!—steer and guide the ship of your life. The leadership of your life is placed solely in your hands. And when you truly set your intentions toward the goal, use your determination and make the effort to reach it, the universe too will provide you a tailwind.

# CHAPTER 3

## Prepare a Life Plan

**Every person should have, at any given moment, a "life plan." Meaning, a prospect of achievements, goals and aims that one wishes to attain. A metaphorical lighthouse of aspirations in different areas which they aspire to reach (and we've already spoken here about the moral lighthouse).**

The goal can be physical as well as spiritual. It may pertain to tangible achievements like gaining wealth, starting a business, an academic degree or attaining a desirable profession, and it may also pertain to realizing a social idea, education, making progress in one's career or to athletic achievements, a new invention, creating, taking a trip, expanding one's family... there are thousands of goals.

It is important that every person have a goal (one or many) in their life, which they wish to realize. When a person sets a goal for themselves, they have a reason to get out of bed in the morning. People who are filled with aspirations have lives that are more meaningful, full of hope, joy, vitality, positive energy and the feeling that they are not futile. They live with a sense of progress according to their own scale of personal needs.

*Rabbi Israel Salanter, founder of the ethics movement in Judaism, said: "Like a bird, man can reach undreamed-of heights as long as he works his wings. Should he relax them for but one minute, however, he plummets downward. Such is man."*

For those who are depressed, who lack vitality and energy, there is no prospect of progress in their lives. They live life simply for the sake of living, they work to earn a living and survive life instead of enjoying it and seeking satisfaction. They go through life without spiritual content, and that's why they are drained energetically. The joy of life was taken from them, and over time they become bitter and frustrated. It is hard to gain their interest, make them happy, or excite them. They face higher health risks than others.

I would suggest to someone who is experiencing a crisis in their life to create a "life plan" for themselves. Every day, when I walk and swim at the beach by my house, I meet a man who sits facing the sea and works on his writing with great diligence. He found his life's calling, even though, apparently, he doesn't gain any social recognition for it.

I would suggest that we all immediately stop doing things in order to gain recognition, certification, attention, appreciation and respect from our environment. This has no real meaning for the person's spirit. True happiness comes from within, by man giving it to himself.

When we reach self-realization and the subjective satisfaction of our spiritual and emotional feelings and needs, and feel that we are moving closer to the goal we set for ourselves, only then will we feel renewed happiness each and every morning. It has already been stated in our sources that the most important thing in life is the "journey"—the process. Once you have achieved your goal, set a new standard for yourself. Set a new goal for yourself to aspire to.

*As the author Robert Louis Stevenson, said: "Wherever we are, it is but a stage on the way to somewhere else, and whatever we do, however well we do it, it is only a preparation to do something else that shall be different."*

In Alice in Wonderland by Lewis Carroll, Alice asks the Cheshire cat which road she should take. The wise cat responds that if she does not know where she wants to end up, it does not matter which way she goes.

***

If you wish to live a long life, filled with satisfaction and meaning, decide where you want to go, walk the path you chose, and the universe will be with you. A person is alive so long as they still dream. The American poet and author Henry David Thoreau wrote about this: *"Go confidently in the direction of your dreams. Live the life you've imagined."*

# CHAPTER 4

## Take Responsibility for Your Life

**I watched a film that impressed me with its hidden messages. The film portrays the life of Josie Katz, starting from the time she was young, through her miserable period with the talented singer and songwriter Shmulik Kraus, her escape from him, her life in the USA and the tragedy she endured when losing her second husband, until she returned to Israel, her rehabilitation, the new challenges she faced and the way she dealt with them.**

The film clearly shows how the heroine goes through an entire process throughout her life, in which she goes from being a passive woman, the kind whose life is determined by the people around her and the events that occur in her life, to a woman who takes responsibility and leadership over her life. From then on, she was the one leading her life, deciding, initiating, executing, and even paying a price while being aware of the steps she'd take. During her empowerment process, she recognizes her past mistakes, but understands that she could not have understood them earlier, and so she forgives herself. She says "I am no longer mad at anyone, not even myself. Today I understand things that I couldn't have known or understood when I was younger, and this is the natural process."

I agree with this statement, but I believe that it is possible, to some extent, to prepare our children, our students and the youth around us for the understanding of what really matters in life:

- **First of all, we will teach them that only man himself is responsible for his fate and happiness.**

That's why, under no circumstances, should a person put up with a situation where they are suffering physical violence, or emotional violence or both. They must return it in favor, and when there is no choice (for example, when the partner has mental health issues, as in Josie's case) they must simply cut ties, leave or run away. Not reacting to insults, emotional or physical harm, bothersome behavior and violence, will eventually cause these phenomena to intensify. We must understand that if a person close to us behaves this way, the problem is theirs, not ours. It is also important to involve other people in order to receive assistance and break free of this violent relationship.

We must be loyal to ourselves and our truth, and we must never—ever—be silent in the face of violence or aggression. We must not ingratiate ourselves, must not apologize, must not restrain ourselves, must not be nice when it is unnecessary. On the contrary, we must react.

- **We will teach them that we must protect the ones we love.** Protect, meaning trying not to hurt them, cause them harm, defend them physically and emotionally. We must help them if possible, try to make them happy and not cause them any distress. This is true love. People who love their egos more than they love those who are close to them, will eventually find themselves alone.

- **We will teach them to take good advantage of the present and never assume that in the future we will fulfill our dreams.** It is every person's obligation to fulfill their dreams now, in this moment. This is our "money time" and under no circumstances are we to postpone its execution. The past is long gone, and the future is unclear. A person, as a mortal being, does not have an insurance policy for the rest of their lives, and so they must realize their desires, plans and dreams in the present moment.

- **We will teach them to invest in their children's futures.** When people bring children into the world, they have a great moral obligation to invest in them love, attention, and education, and to provide for them respectfully. People who, for whatever reason, cannot fulfill their duties as parents (mostly for emotional reasons, not economical) should do the ethical thing and not have children. Bringing children into a world of suffering, emotional distress, great pain and trauma is a double sin. How will a person who cannot "carry" themselves emotionally and physically, also "carry" their children?

Another message that I liked in the film was Josie's statement about her desire for a man who will love her more than she loves him. She's tired of being the victim, giving of herself and receiving a beating in return. She wants to feel courted, loved, desired. She wants to be encouraged, complemented, appreciated for her actions, not the contrary.

Josie turned her emotional distress into creation, and she did so in a way that warrants respect. The creative channel as a tool for healing, raising our consciousness, releasing frustration, anger, thoughts and also joy—is an excellent tool, which is beneficial for all of us.

Many people begin creating at later stages in their lives, and to their great benefit. When you create, and it doesn't matter what, do not think at all about the marketing and turning it outwards. Think instead about the contribution of this creation to your spirit and about the messages that come up through your work. This is a tool for purification, for cleaning and airing out emotions, for expressing opinions and for crying out. A tool for defiance, shouting and protest.

Another point that was made in the film is the need for only taking personal responsibility. We cannot take responsibility for someone else and feel guilty, or alternatively, feel pleased with someone else's behavior. Moreover, our behavior should not be influenced at all by the actions of others, their words or the messages they try to send us. Our backbone is built solely on our own truth, and so it is irrelevant what another person says or does, even if they are close to us. We take responsibility only for our own actions. This way, we will feel "lighter," guilt-free and unapologetic.

***

It isn't "mine," it's "his" or "hers." Simply put. Just as the heroine of the film says: "Why are you asking me how he feels? Ask him!"

# CHAPTER 5

## Live a Life of Meaning

**Every one of us has aspirations, desires and dreams which are like a lighthouse that lights up our lives. That is where we aspire to go. The lighthouse lights our path in the darkness (which is a metaphor for life's difficulties, internal and external blocks, the hesitations and the deliberations we encounter at crucial points in our lives). A person's lighthouse that is tall, high, upright and clear—its light will also be bright, sharp, straight and with a clear direction. The light isn't scattered but focused.**

A person with no lighthouse, which acts as a practical and moral compass, will have a hard time achieving professional, social and personal goals. For the most part, their lives will be directionless and they will act in a technical manner, without any emotional connection to their aspirations and desires. They will live their lives out of necessity for income and will survive the waves of life without an emotional anchor to provide internal support and an internal control center. When deeds and actions are disconnected from the soul, they are not powerful and not meaningful.

*Walt Disney said: "A person should set his goals as early as he can and devote all his energy and talent to getting there."*

*And yet the German philosopher Friedrich Nietzsche said: "He who has a why to live can bear almost any how."*

People who haven't clarified for themselves the meaning of their lives, the values that are important to them, the goals they wish to achieve and their priorities, will experience  emotional fatigue, exhaustion and lack of vitality. This process takes place when the connection is missing between the soul, the body and the reality of life. Instead of feeling unity of body and soul, they will mostly feel sadness and frustration and will miss the joy of creation and the joy of discovery. They will not express their innate creative abilities, and are instead likened to a flower whose petals are closed. They will be lackluster people and so their body will respond accordingly. They will suffer from different health issues and emotional issues. They will feel worn out and their immune system will be weakened.

*According to the Austrian-British philosopher Ludwig Wittgenstein, if we can find the meaning of life and the world – we can call that meaning God.*

*** 

When People identify feelings of fatigue and exhaustion, they are obligated to strengthen themselves, take care of their consciousness and create goals and destinations for their lives that will guide and light their way. They must strengthen their inner lighthouse through spiritual work. This process in itself will provide healing for body and spirit.

# CHAPTER 6

## Don't Worship the "Golden Calf"

**There are people who mistakenly believe that setting a goal in life will enslave them and their entire being in order to achieve this goal, and that it is therefore dangerous. It can be argued that this claim is true if the person turns their life goal into an existential "golden calf." In this case, the goal is in control of them, they are not in control of their goal.**

It is clear to everyone that setting goals in life gives our life meaning. A person must set short-term and long-term goals for themselves—a kind of lighthouse for life, a direction to aspire to and place their efforts. Devoting ourselves to such goals will give life its valuable and moral purpose and fill our spirits with passion and energy.

*The pioneer and philosopher A.D Gordon, who was a spiritual teacher for the youth that came to the Land of Israel in the early 20th century, demonstrated this in the sentence: "You must attain life while living, because life is life, because life is creating."*

Many wise people have already said that the journey is more important than the goal. The patient and focused work, step after step while skipping over life's obstacles and occasional difficulties—invites opportunities for us to learn something about ourselves and others. Along the way, we will express our talents, creations, resourcefulness and joyful creativity. In the process, we will also express other important qualities, like self-restraint, patience, discernment, persistence, determination and more. Reaching our final destination will fill us with feelings of satisfaction, pride and happiness. It will give us confidence, and raise our spirits, thanks to us using our abilities and overcoming obstacles and hurdles (And yet, it is best if every endpoint will also be a starting point for a new challenge. We must not sit idly by our achievements. The constant creativity and personal developments are important so we know that we haven't wasted our lives and that they had meaning and accomplishments).

*In this context, let's read the words of Eleanor Roosevelt, wife of US president Franklin Delano Roosevelt, and also diplomat, politician and human rights activist: "The future belongs to those who believe in the beauty of their dreams."*

Unfortunately, many people raise their careers, money, education and prestige to the utmost importance in their lives. They sanctify it and convey this to their children and environment. Throughout life, they become their own victims by sacrificing their lives, attention, time and family on the altar of the goal they worship.

There is nothing in life worth turning into a golden calf, meaning a goal above everything else in our lives, if on that same golden calf altar we would sacrifice our family and loved ones. Investing in our beloved family is the most important thing. In the end, worshiping profitable material values and achievements is like a boomerang that harms the person.

People that are addicted to their jobs / to making a fortune / to success in business / to their career (even more so when talking about addiction to alcohol, drugs, sex), repeatedly lose sight of the stopping point and the point of no return. When one's personal brakes do not work, it means that the person loses their boundaries, their restraints and the correct proportions for life. After a while, they may discover that neglecting their family brought on disastrous repercussions, sometimes divorce, neglected children who use drugs as an escape, alienation between them and their children to the point of causing a rift, and many other repercussions that will be very hard to fix.

Let us return to the old familiar mantra: balance is the keyword for a good life. We live better while consciously knowing that we must find balance between the necessities of our careers, our family and our spirit, for balance is the basis for a life filled with the sense of emotional calm and being at peace with who I am, with the environment (professional, social and personal) and with what is required of me as a complete person.

My intention is not that our lives will become perfect, since there is no such thing as a perfect life, and there is no need for it to be so. Perfection is reserved for imaginary gods. We better not get lost in the delusion that somewhere out there, on the horizon or in the future, we can lay back on a bed of roses and finally live the life of our dreams. We must begin in this very moment to live the lives that we dream about.

\*\*\*

Let us learn to not stretch our limitations to the edge of our abilities. In any area. If we do not go to the edge on any topic in our lives, and definitely not at the expense of other areas, our chances improve for living a life of happiness, self-fulfillment and satisfaction.

# SECTION 2

FREEDOM

# CHAPTER 7

# Abolish the Imaginary Blocks in Your Mind

**A border is a line that we draw physically, symbolically, intellectually or consciously, and in Hebrew, the word shares the same root as the verb "to limit" and "limitation."**

We are all in need of boundaries in our daily behavior and conduct—for ourselves and for the world. Boundaries are our human restraints and the brakes that we place in every area of our lives. We place boundaries for ourselves and others according to our values, priorities, physical and emotional strengths, and our sensitivities and needs.

Human society has set codes of conducts and norms that are unwritten but are basic in the lives of humans, and are thus learned through the process of socialization. Children learn from a very young age what the boundaries are and even constantly check the limits of what is allowed and what is forbidden. Placing boundaries and respecting them is an important part of the educational process.

Unconsciously, many people set limits for themselves also in their minds: how far they can reach. However, by placing these limits within our imagination and consciousness, we limit our ability to attain achievements in advance. This happens because our consciousness is not in sync with our aspirations and it sends us negative messages about our ability to reach goals and objectives.

Many of us possess thought patterns that limit us. We often operate on auto-pilot—meaning, in the ways that we are used to operating in—instead of asking ourselves why we do the things we do and not otherwise. It is entirely possible that we could have acted differently and reached different and better results. Thought patterns hold us in place and limit us.

*Franklin Delano Roosevelt, former US president, defined it well in this sentence: "Men are not prisoners of fate, but only prisoners of their own minds." And Abraham Lincoln said: "Always bear in mind that your own resolution to succeed is more important than any other."*

*Rabbi Shlomo Yitzchaki, 1040-1105, one of the greatest commentators on the Old Testament and Talmud, said: "Along the way that a man wants to go, on it he is taken."*

*Harriet Tubman, American abolitionist, who escaped slavery and led 13 missions to free 70 slaves, said: "Every great dream begins with a dreamer. Always remember, you have within you the strength, the patience, and the passion to reach for the stars to change the world."*

Many people are afraid of being unordinary or unusual. They are afraid of making moves that will raise eyebrows or cause laughter among their social circles, and so they abide by limiting social norms, which very often castrates them and blocks their creativity. It is important to remember that the people who do unconventional things, are the ones who will eventually obtain unconventional achievements.

This is why change and growth begin with breaking through boundaries of thought and consciousness. The moment we see ourselves as if in the position and place we want to be, then we have already completed half the journey.

* The first change will be made in our consciousness. We must start thinking "naturally," as if it is obvious that we will get to where we want to go. From here, processes will be easier, since the universe too will provide support. Remember: When people actually set their intentions toward a goal, so too will the forces of the universe and nature join together with their desires and the actions that they are taking.

* Do not rush straight to the end. Divide the overall mission into smaller steps and outline sub-stages. Our greatest difficulty usually lies in the first steps. Many people get "cold feet" when they want to begin a process of change. Remember: The moment you take the first steps, things will flow naturally. In the armed corps, it is customary to say: Things work out while you're in motion.

Never give up trying to fulfill your dreams. It is important that we are in midst of a flow, that we begin processes. Passivity is more dangerous than a faulty step. It keeps us in place, nails us down to an unwanted reality.

***

In order to make positive changes in life and obtain achievements, we must first imagine that we are in that desired place and then take steps and actions in order to achieve them. This is also how we will receive support and backup from the universe. And most importantly, have no fear.

# CHAPTER 8

# Release Your Inner Chains

**Enslavement is first and foremost an emotional state, a state of mind. The chains in our lives are internal chains, like a glass ceiling that exists within us, and they stop us from realizing ourselves and reaching our fullest unique and powerful potential. Enslavement is a bondage that we take upon ourselves, of our own free will. Enslavement is a choice.**

Contrarily, the meaning of freedom—on a personal, emotional and spiritual level—is when the person acts as their own light. Osho, the Indian spiritual teacher, said: "One's own personal inner darkness is preferable to the light of another person." And our sages said: "If I am not for me, who will be for me?" It is every person's responsibility to find their inner light without relying on other people (including spiritual teachers) to fill themselves with the energies of life and joy.

Freedom is releasing the inner chains that block us: anxieties, fears, feelings of guilt, fear of social sanctions. Freedom is the possibility to act and live according to a "personal Everest" and not a "Social Everest." Freedom means living according to our truth. Freedom is the right to be who we are, in all our human complexity, our memories, the scars that left their mark on our psyches and the empowering experiences alongside the frustrations and disappointments.

Memorize the following:

- **Real freedom** is the ability to identify the people that weaken us and stay away from them, just as it is the ability to connect with people who strengthen and empower us.

- **Real freedom** is the choice that we make in our own unique way, of walking down the path of our truth and not what is socially acceptable, in every area of our lives.

- **Real freedom** is the freedom of thought and the right to be free of tyranny, physical or emotional slavery, hidden or overt; the kind hiding behind slogans or manipulations and kept concealed in clever ways. Real freedom is the freedom of expression and criticism.

- **Real freedom** is freedom that a person takes for themselves and does not wait for it to be given by someone else. Meaning: being the one leading their own life and not being led by others.

- **Real freedom** is the ability to let go of anything that is irrelevant to our lives in the present: people, feelings of guilt, regrets over things we did wrong in the past, memories, places, feelings of anger, life situations—and allow it to evaporate from our lives.

- **Real freedom** is the decision to live in the present moment and not let the past control us. Leaving the past in the past.

- **Real freedom** is the right to be at peace with who we are and to love ourselves.

***

I wish all of us a life of personal freedom.

# CHAPTER 9

# Live Life Without Fear and Worry

Personal freedom is an abstract concept, with broad definitions and a deep meaning that manifests in many areas. Thanks to this freedom, a person gives themselves the legitimacy to be loyal to who they are, their worldviews, values and personality. They are authentic and honest first and foremost to themselves. They have the courage and wisdom to "dig" into their values and belief systems, identify and remove perceptions and social codes that they absorbed over the years and which overshadowed their inner essence. They feel free "to peel" them away without any misgivings, due to the understanding that only without them will they be able to be loyal to themselves and fully act out their qualities, preferences and skills.

*In his book, "The Reveries of a Solitary Walker," the philosopher Jean-Jacques Rousseau, wrote: "The habit of retiring within myself, made me soon lose the feeling, and almost the remembrance of my sorrows; thus I learned, by my own experience, that the source of true happiness is in ourselves, and that it is beyond the power of man to render those truly miserable, who determine to be otherwise."*

The concept of emotional freedom includes within it the freedom of thought. Removing the shells that cover the consciousness involve also removing axioms of thought, which are considered "absolute truths" and were born as a result of education and messages embedded in us over the years. Without these shells, a person can develop independent creative thinking, critical thinking and judgment of reality, without fearing social criticism. Freedom of thought provides the legitimacy and courage to express opinions that do not align with the hegemonic narrative, and to go against the mainstream.

Personal freedom means that a person is free to accept and love themselves as they are. Living with a disguise and a persona that does not express a person's true qualities, takes a heavy emotional toll. The work required for creating an external image, a brand, which is directed outward, robs us of the emotional energy that could have been used for creating, for utilizing one's artistic abilities, for personal development, for deriving pleasure from what is, and for growth. All the things that bring happiness and spiritual perfection.

The person who arrives at inner freedom will discover that conducting oneself without disguises, pretenses, hypocrisy and manipulating words, is the correct way of conduct, which in the long run will bring real positive results. Timeless results. This type of conduct will enable them to reach artistic accomplishments, ground-breaking results in academic fields and research and originality in every area of their life. A person who is not chained to conventions, can be ground-breaking in their field and in any route they choose.

As long as a person is alive, and are in sync with their human core, and act in accordance with their human spark within and the qualities and qualifications they are born with—they can reach happiness. A person who lives under "shells" and disguises, cannot reach self-fulfillment and happiness.

*Steve Jobs, founder of Apple computer company, defined this well in his speech for Stanford graduates in 2005: "Don't let the noise of others' opinions drown out your own inner voice."*

However, in order to fully live in a state of personal freedom, you must be equipped with emotional strength and courage. A person who chooses to be different and unusual in their ways, is often subject to criticism and social sanctions. Personal freedom may sometimes mean loneliness and social isolation, insult and shaming.

The internet and the various social networks of our times have become instruments that express the voice of the crowd, a sort of modern "town square," since it is a legitimate and free arena for every person to express their opinions. This is the essence of democracy and it gives the public the possibility to influence the political, cultural and social life of the society and state. However, the internet carries some danger, since people who express different opinions attract shaming. The internet has become a violent arena of slander, fake news and unrestrained tongue-lashing directed at those whose opinions are not liked by others.

*This is exactly what Henrik Ibsen, the Norwegian playwright, meant when he wrote: "Public opinion is an extremely mutable thing."*

*And Gustave Le Bon, French psychologist and author, said: "How great is the number of men whose opinions have never differed from those in the newspapers."*

And yet, in spite of the verbal violence on social networks, it is important that one can express their opinions without fear. It's true, people are vulnerable to social sanctions instigated against those who go against the mainstream, but if they choose to be a conformist, they won't have any breakthroughs in life. They will constantly live in a state of giving up: giving up on their unique voice being heard, giving up on utilizing their talents, giving up on themselves (it is important to note that expressing one's inner truth does not legitimize insulting or shaming another person. Criticism must always be topical and backed up with facts).

A person's true happiness is attained when they express who they are in an absolute manner, when they give up the desire to be like someone else or embrace qualities that are not in their personal arsenal.

*The American philosopher and author Ralph Waldo Emerson, of the 19th century, defined it well: "To be yourself in a world that is constantly trying to make you something else, is the greatest accomplishment."*

When a person makes peace with who they are, they lovingly accept themselves with all their uniqueness and shortcomings and they are at peace with their personality, character and abilities. From that point, they must strive to fulfill their purpose on this planet. Making peace with who we are, will enable us to fully realize the good within us, for our own good, the good of those around us and the whole of society.

In each one of us there is a divine spark, a piece of the universe that is the core of our lives, and therein lie our innate talents and basic personality traits. And still, we are not always satisfied. This is how, for example, a naturally shy and introverted person might adopt some social mannerisms, but the characteristics of their personality will not change, and over the years they will torment themselves over not moving into the center of the stage and letting others pick the fruits of their labor. A person like this will do good to use external sources and professionals who know the art of marketing. Sometimes, also a personal coach can help them empower less prominent parts of their professional conduct.

It is important that we first love ourselves. In the Raja Yoga guidebook, it is written that a person must have a connection with four elements in their lives: first of all, with silence.

They must be able to be in silence and feel the flow of life, the size of the universe and their place within it. The second connection is with themselves. They must love themselves and accept themselves as they are and never be critical of themselves. Thirdly, they must be connected with the Creator of the universe, and only fourth and last, they must be connected with the people around them.

***

This perspective fits in well with what was written: before anything else, a person must live in peace and love with themselves and who they are. A person who does not love themselves, all their qualities and shortcomings included, is not capable of loving others. A person who cannot forgive themselves, cannot forgive others. A person who is not demanding of themselves, will not be demanding of others. And so on.

# CHAPTER 10

## Rely on Your Inner Anchor

**Physical and emotional independence gives a person confidence and power. They become their own anchor, for both their lives and their personality.**

This does not mean that a person must live in a bubble that is disconnected from social ties. On the contrary, relationships with others are one of the most important and empowering stages in a person's life, and they allow us to give of our light to others and simultaneously receive from them. Our whole lives are based on the constant conversation and vital interaction with our surroundings, and yet, we must not rely on social connections in order to live a joyful life, with satisfaction and energy from within. We must build for ourselves a personal anchor, so that we do not, heaven forbid, be a burden to others: children, acquaintances, friends or neighbors. At any age, we must build around us a supportive social circle and meaningful life systems, which include hobbies, learning, volunteering and other activities.

*The German poet, playwright and philosopher, Friedrich Schiller said: "Be noble minded! Our own heart, and not other men's opinions of us, forms our true honor."*

Sometimes, also those close to us and loved ones use (whether consciously or unconsciously) emotional manipulations on those around them, so they will pity them and devote more attention to them. However, casting the responsibility on to others, and demanding that they fill our lives with content and interest, is entirely unfair. Those closest to us, as loved as they may be, cannot and should not accept responsibility and control over our lives. They are living their lives on the path that they chose for themselves, and we are marching down our own life's path. Putting pressure on others (covert or overt) by using feelings of guilt and manipulations, and all this so that they will devote more time and attention to us, is an ugly and despicable act.

And what about older parents and children? Our sages have said about this: "Cast me not off in the time of old age" and also "Honor your father and your mother." It is important that we learn to identify the thin line between the desire and need to take care of our parents who need us and assist them in whatever is necessary, and the emotional urge to please them and quiet our own guilt feelings. And like everything else in life, it is important that here too, we must find the balance between investing quality time in the family of our own that we started, and investing time and emotional energy in our relatives who need us, too.

A grown man that loves his grown children, takes care of their emotional welfare, and has the sense of decency, will allow them to find their way to him on their own, and will not torment them with the whipping and stabbing of guilty feelings. If he has done his job as parent properly, educated and loved his children, he should trust that they will take care of him in his later years without making it a guilt-ridden chore; rather the children will do it naturally and easily, as an inseparable part of a healthy life.

*As Poet and author James Oppenheim said: "The foolish man seeks happiness in the distance. The wise grows it under his feet."*

\*\*\*

Remember: The key to internal emotional happiness, at any age, is in our hands and not anything external.

# CHAPTER 11

# Manage Only Yourselves

**Emotional manipulations do not stay just in the family. Many people around us use different manipulations on those around them, so they will act as they de sire and according to their own needs and interests. They will plant feelings of guilt in others as if they did not treat them like they should be treated, or paint themselves as "victims" or "weaklings" in order to get attention, pity, consideration, concessions and more. In this case, the weakness becomes the power and instrument to achieve goals.**

The attempt to manage people through manipulations comes from the desire to control the way they behave, turn them into slaves (emotionally, of course), and therefore this action is unacceptable from its core.

"Selfishness" and loving yourself are not negative things. Selfishness is subjective in the eyes of the observer, but many people use this word manipulatively for their own needs. They convey to others that they are "selfish" so they will feel guilty for not fulfilling commitments that are supposedly expected of them, and in this way they turn them into "slaves" in the emotional sense. They enslave them and control them for their needs, and manage their lives. In fact, by using the word "selfish" they say: "You are not doing enough for us."

There are other negative ways of weakening others: Sending hidden or open messages to people that they are not successful, not worthy, stupid, lack abilities or skills. Sometimes, self-aggrandization is also added to these hidden messages. While invalidating the personality of the other, they also boast freely about their own personal accomplishments.

This is the way that certain people weaken and lower those that threaten them (in their own minds) and elevate themselves. In many cases, these corrupt ways stem from lack of self-confidence and jealousy of the success or talents of others. It is best to be aware of this despised strategy and not cooperate with it. It is important not to be dragged into an argument with them, because this confrontation will bring out negative energy from us that will drain us for some time and prevent us from making progress, creating and flourishing. These people succeed in planting in us feelings of discomfort, inferiority, unworthiness, while in reality—that is exactly how they feel about themselves. Eleanor Roosevelt, former First Lady of the United States, said about this: *"No one can make you feel inferior without your consent."*

The need to belittle others exists in people who suffer from inferiority themselves. That is their way of letting out frustration and lack of confidence. A person confident in themselves and their abilities, will not feel the need to belittle other people. They will not feel threatened by others, or be jealous of others' success. Only people who are frustrated with their lives wish to hurt and harm others. Several years ago, I heard a smart saying about this: "Unpleasant people are people who don't have it pleasant."

*Rabbi Nachman from Breslov said: "Always wear a smile. The gift of life will then be yours to give. Sometimes, people are terribly distressed, but have no one to whom they can unburden themselves. If you come alone with a happy face, you cheer them and give them new life."*

Every person is reserved the freedom to live their lives according to their understanding, their physical and emotional strengths, needs, values and priorities. From time to time, I think about my late grandmother, Grandma Eva, who especially loved spending time with her grandchildren and talking with them, but never gave us the feeling that she was resentful of us because we didn't call her enough, didn't visit her as she expected or for "neglecting" her. She always said, "I'm so happy you called" or, "You made me so happy by coming to visit me. Do it a lot..." and she never said this with a reprimanding tone or with blame, so heaven forbid it wouldn't come across as: "You are in the wrong, you neglected me." For this reason, she was very loved by the family. They always felt wonderful around her. She gave everyone the feeling that visiting her was a wonderful gift, and so visiting her was always done with great fun and pleasure, and was never accompanied with the sense of fulfilling an obligation.

Let us not give those around us the feeling that we expect something of them. Our only expectation should be from ourselves and in co-ordination with our partners. Even if friends disappoint us in certain situations, it is best to broach the subject in an honest and friendly conversation, but not go and accuse them with: "You are wrong."

And by the way, I would suggest that every one of us check in with themselves about why they are in a relationship with these kinds of people:

- Does the relationship nourish them on an emotional level and does it exist without any pretenses?

- And perhaps the relationship exists out of inertia, a relationship that began long ago, that makes you uncomfortable at the thought of cutting ties?

And in general, I would suggest we all get rid of the phrase "uncomfortable." We must do what we feel is in accordance with our truth. Our time is valuable and so is our emotional energy.

*** 

Let us decide that from now on, we are preserving our relationships with friends dear to us who nourish us emotionally, friends who are loyal and fun to be around and ones we can trust. If they do not answer these criteria, maybe we should consider cutting ties with them.

# CHAPTER 12

# A Few Words on Integrity

**Integrity, according to the dictionary, is the quality of being honest and having strong moral principles; moral uprightness. Integrity means living according to an inner sense of honesty, fairness to oneself and one's surroundings. But the deeper definition of this term is being loyal to your principles in any situation.**

*The philosopher Jean-Jacques Rousseau wrote in his book "The Reveries of a Solitary Walker": "Innocence is the only support I depend on in my sufferings, how much more wretched then should I make myself, if relinquishing this last, this powerful resource, I substituted wickedness in its place?"*

It isn't so brave being loyal to one's principles when a person has no financial stresses or existential danger. The difficulty begins when your life's foundation is destabilized. When the threat of financial collapse or a threat to personal safety hangs over you and your family; when you are under attack at the front lines of your job, business or political or academic activism; when you are lonely or when your health is at risk.

It is possible you will aspire to reach a certain goal but all your honest attempts at reaching it were unsuccessful. At this point, you may decide, consciously or as a temporary fix (so you tell yourself), to give up your integrity. This means that you never had integrity to begin with. The moral principles were never impressed upon your personality and were not really a part of you. Best case scenario, they served as decor, a placard for marketing and branding purposes. At times, not even that. So long as your life was working well, you didn't use lies and manipulations because you didn't need them. The first instant in which you act in corrupt ways in order to attain your goal, you begin digging your own grave.

There isn't a person in the world who can corrupt you but yourself. A person who is not equipped with a solid and moral backbone, a person lacking a strong and stable moral compass, is doomed to lose their way even if they have succeeded in climbing the social, professional and financial ladders. If along the way they were able to achieve their goals by lying and manipulating, this will not last forever. At some point in their lives, their corrupt ways will be exposed and they will pay the price for it.

According to the Dalai Lama, strong people, too—people who supposedly have complete control over their lives, such as wealthy people, businessmen and politicians—they and others like them are also dependent on other people. Their power and accomplishments came to them from others. This means, that a person must forever be equipped with qualities of compassion and love for their fellow man: love for themselves, the people around them, and the universe. They must see themselves as a part of society and a universe that they are connected to and obligated to. And so they must feel a constant sense of gratitude: for their lives, their family, their profession and place of work. Gratitude for their home, health, fortune, friends and all their life's achievements.

A person must love others to the same extent that they love themselves. Try this technique: try and step into someone else's shoes. Imagine yourselves entering someone's soul and feeling their feelings. This will teach you to see others as subjects (not objects) with emotions, desires, wishes, passions, fears and aspirations. This way, you will learn something about their motives, and also about your own.

This exercise will teach you to treat others with the respect they deserve, and it doesn't matter what their profession, social status, religion, gender and so on is. They are also souls like you. They also have the right to live on this earth and find happiness like you. They may be rivals in business, politics, colleagues competing at your place of work or in sports, people competing for the same territory—we must get accustomed to seeing them as human beings without labels and stereotypes. We must try to understand the entirety of their motives, and then, perhaps, we will succeed in settling our disputes.

I feel great shame when faced with racist jokes, or jokes that taint and shame entire communities. This is, to my understanding, the deeper meaning of humanity: the realization that we are all made up of one big human fabric whose source is in the heart of the universe. This means that we are all on the same physical and material level.

\*\*\*

Our spiritual level will be determined by us. This is where we have a choice. As human beings, we have the responsibility to make progress throughout our lives to a higher level of spirituality and morality. Every person should see themselves as a spiritual guide for their children, friends and community. A guide that does not come from above or with arrogance, but remains at eye level. Show others a different way of seeing things.

# CHAPTER 13

# Getting Offended is Giving Your Power to Another

**Getting offended means attributing to someone else the ability and power to harm us. Getting offended means being defeated, losing the battle and feeling exhausted and drained of energy. Getting offended means letting another person influence our lives and emotional state.**

Let us look at this from another angle: who is that person that I should even be offended by them? Are they among my close friends? One of my family members? A co-worker? Do they surpass me in their human qualities and attributes? Are they more talented or important than I am? And assuming that according to professional hierarchy they are above me—so what?

If they act in a way that offends me, in an ugly manner that does not hold up to my moral standards, with maliciousness, tactlessness—it is a testimony to a flaw in them, not me. I do not need the stamp of approval from any person on earth, any organization, to know that I am full of human qualities. I do not need a good word to know what I am worth and what my value is. I do not need a certificate from anyone. I will give myself my own certificate. It is enough that I know this and believe it with all my heart.

*Aristotle wrote about this: "There is only one way to avoid criticism: do nothing, say nothing and be nothing."*

We better stay away from people who are bitter, frustrated and flaky, those who make us feel bad about ourselves; people who cause us feelings of guilt, distress, anger, depression. If these are our "friends," we'd better cut off ties with them. And if they are family—we must reduce our connection with them and keep it to a minimum.

Let us take it further and say that no person in the world is superior to us or surpasses us in any area, even if they are wealthier than us, more important professionally, better educated, stronger, prettier and so on. All human beings were created equal and no one person has the moral right to rise above another person for whatever reason. If they do behave this way, their behavior is worthy of condemnation.

A person's status in society is determined only by their own feeling, the way they see themselves and the self-esteem they have for themselves. A person who chooses to feel poor, like a victim, weak and miserable, will indeed have a matching personal and social standing and they will feel bitter all their lives.

*The author and social activist, Helen Keller, who was deaf, blind and mute said: "When one door of happiness closes, another opens, but often we look so long at the closed door that we do not see the one that has been opened for us."*

A person who decides that they are full of humane and professional qualities, who is convinced that they are a "human power plant" and can share their light with others, will feel throughout their lives that their happiness is in their hands. They will discover in every corner of their lives a bit of happiness, will ignore negative energy around them and feel fully that their lives are full of self-fulfillment. The certifications that human society gives us, such as money, status, jobs, prestige—they have nothing on happiness. Happiness is a subjective feeling that exists independently of our social status or profession. It is hidden in the smallest treasure chests of life, and so it is important that every person identify these chests that grant them joy and happiness.

***

In each and every moment remember that you are the kings of your life. In life, choose to be kings.

# CHAPTER 14

# Don't Believe Everything They Say About You

**David Ben-Gurion once said: "Our future depends not on what the gentiles will say, but on what the Jews will do!" This statement is true even more so for the individual. It was very lucky for the Jewish People that Binyamin Ze'ev Herzl, visionary of the Jewish state, did not pay attention to all the criticism and ridicule that his opposition threw at him. He believed in his path and established the Zionist movement almost from nothing, and the rest is history...**

It is important to repeat this again and again, since we, as human beings tend to lose faith in our ways and in ourselves because of the reactions of our surroundings. We need positive external feedback in order to progress on the path we believe in, and it is important to reiterate that this is meaningless. It does not matter at all what so and so will say, or even what our friends will say. Ignore what others say and think about you, even those you consider your friends and well-wishers. Following the command of your conscience is what matters.

*Actor Johnny Depp said: "Do what you really want to do. Don't play their game! Don't do what they want. Find your own way."*

This is all the more important when the fuel of our critics comes from jealousy, envy and maliciousness. Make yourselves as if blind and deaf, imagine that you are like the donkey, whose eyes are blindfolded as he walks along a cliff—and move forward on the path you chose. Do not respond to the insults and evil words, which are sometimes thrown at you by envious, mean-spirited people.

I'll take it a step further: sometimes, even our parents and other loved ones will oppose the personal or professional path we choose. Assuming we don't choose a destructive path for ourselves, we must choose one that matches our heart's desire. If there is something we wish to do with our whole heart and soul and with passion—we must do it, even if our close surroundings will raise their eyebrows (all this, of course, as long as it does not harm us or other people, especially those dear to us).

What do I mean? Here are some examples: a young man decides to become religious, against the wishes of his secular parents. Another person chooses a profession that isn't so profitable, but one that is satisfying and gives them a sense of purpose. A third person decides not to go to university and instead open an independent business that they believe in. Everyone has the right to follow their heart's calling.

Every person has the basic responsibility of providing for their children, give them warmth and love, educate and guide them until they have matured. A person cannot disregard these obligations in the name of their personal desires. When one brings children into the world, one must know that this is a long-term commitment. If so, when we want to fulfill our goals, we cannot ignore the personal commitments that we took upon ourselves as parents, but this doesn't mean we have to give up on our dreams. We must look for any possibility of actualizing them.

There are people who do not fulfill their needs emotionally, professionally and spiritually, instead their life course is determined by the current social climate. Usually, this is the result of education and messages according to which one must fall in line with social norms, not stand out in any way, say the "right" thing, and do the "right" thing. In short, walk the line of limitations that society places on us.

I would like to request that everyone test themselves with the following questions:
* What is the significance of the fact that my actions "look good" in the eyes of others?
* Does this have any influence on my quality of life, success, happiness, etc.?

What would be the benefit for each of us, if the people around us (and I am purposefully using this vague term, since our actions are not directed at a specific public, and this emphasizes even more, the pointlessness and stupidity in this line of thinking) would think and even say about us that we are "OK." That we are good, smart, and talented, behave with decency, are successful etc. After all, it is never – not even once! - possible to please the whole public. Any attempt at such is doomed to fail.

*The journalist and publicist Herbert Bayard Swope said about this: "I can't give you a sure-fire formula for success, but I can give you a formula for failure: try to please everybody all the time."*

What benefit will we gain if the people around us think we are good-looking, talented and successful, and say so, but we, deep down, feel miserable and unsatisfied?

What matters is our own feelings in regard to ourselves and life. It's important that we live our lives according to our inner truth and not according to social orders.

The physician, psychiatrist and Holocaust survivor, Viktor Frankl, believed that within every man is spiritual freedom. In his book, Man's Search for Meaning, he wrote that the freedom of thought, which creates significance and meaning and leads one throughout life – and that no man has the right to deny this in another.

We must only serve our soul and our emotional and intellectual needs. What will determine our quality of life and happiness, is the extent to which we will utilize our abilities and live in peace and harmony with ourselves. The constant attempt to please others and win external validation will cause us to live in constant lack and with the feeling that we are not good enough in relation to others. We must remember at any given moment that we are whole, full and good—the moment we are good to ourselves.

It is important that we learn not to compare our lives with the lives of others. Usually, we only see the tip of the iceberg of the lives of those around us. But we must remember that "the grass is always greener on the other side" and "not all that glitters is gold." Happiness and the real meaning of life is living in peace with ourselves and loving who we are; living with the flow of life, without feeling guilty and without feeling that we are missing something, but that we are whole.

This does not mean that we shouldn't strive to reach personal and professional achievements. Many of those who attain these achievements do so out of the desire to win social respect and appreciation. There is nothing wrong with that, as long as the person stays loyal to their true self, and does not forget to place themselves before society and their surroundings. A person who enslaves themselves, their feelings and their soul in order to gain respect, prestige and recognition, are deserving of pity. They will never be at peace and have self-love for who they are, and this will cause them to continue proving themselves to themselves.

Oftentimes, this conduct stems from lack of self-confidence and the desire to lean on external figures who will "validate" our abilities, instead of an inner foundation of believing in ourselves.

A person must bring forth into the world their innate abilities, without fearing social criticism. The American author Theodor Seuss Geisel (aka Dr. Seuss) phrased it this way: *"Why fit in when you were born to stand out?"*

A person who lives in fear of being different and unordinary, will be afraid to break boundaries. In order to attain unusual achievements, we must carry out unusual actions. In order to create innovation and freshness, we must break boundaries. If we fear the reactions of others, we will not write, create, innovate; we will not express an opinion and we will not break boundaries of intellect and consciousness.

*Former US president, Theodore Roosevelt said about this: "The only thing we have to fear is fear itself."*

A person who is truly free must be liberated from prejudices and the fear of "what will they say?" This is the true power that will open doors for them: doors of progress beyond routine, beyond the ordinary and expected, and beyond the norm. In order to create new things, courage is necessary to withstand the criticism of the environment. The courage to withstand ridicule, laughter, sometimes ostracism. The greatest creators in history, from the founder of Christianity to the founders of the feminist movement—suffered from humiliation and social contempt, and they got through it thanks to the strong faith in the righteousness of their paths.

What distinguishes them is their faith in their path and the willingness to stand up for themselves, for their opinions, for their creation opposite the surrounding society. Fame usually comes later, and often, this ground-breaking person is no longer alive to enjoy it and free themselves of the shame of humiliation.

*** 

*Remember the words of philosopher Ralph Waldo Emerson: "The only person you are destined to become, is the person you decide to be. Walk down the path you believe in."*

# CHAPTER 15

## It's Not Okay!

**We were all raised with the values of tidiness and cleanliness. Every one of us adopted these principles (to different extents) and tries to uphold them in our day-to-day lives. However, I am here to try and disprove this social axiom. In my opinion, exaggeration about being clean and tidy is negative and bad, just as any other quality that is taken to the extreme.**

Now you must be asking: Who is this bad for? The person themselves? For society? Their surroundings? I won't be going out on a limb by saying that a person who is too clean, too tidy, who demands the same level of cleanliness from their surroundings (family, co-workers), might dampen the mood wherever they go. They will feel stressed out, ruin their own mood, and harm the sense of peace and comfort of those around him.

Over-meticulousness in these two areas of tidiness and cleanliness might be an indicator of some emotional problem, for example suppressed anger, fear, or lack of confidence. Our personal safety does not depend on the order around us (although order does contribute to our sense of calm). Whoever goes crazy when their home is not as tidy as a museum, will benefit from seeking treatment to find their inner order and balance, in their "inner home." Our inner balance should not depend on whether the objects in our house are in their rightful place.

I'll take it a step further. In my opinion, over-meticulousness about order, setting an exact place and function for each item, blocks our creativity. This meticulousness places limitations where there should be openness and space. A little mess, a little untidiness that can be controlled, the mixing of different fields—might actually inspire one's mind. In a place where there are no blocks and no boundaries of fields, everything is open. All possibilities are open. While separating different fields and placing physical objects (which are a metaphor for ideas and fields of knowledge) into drawers, is artificial and limiting for thought and creativity.

A creative person must create in an environment of freedom, of mixing fields, of calmness, of blurry boundaries, of stretching limitations. Order that is too rigid might be a sign of dogmatic thinking. Aesthetic order and perfection give us security, but trap us in a prison of mind and consciousness that is bordered with artificial and unnecessary boundaries.

*"It is better to live in your own destiny imperfectly than to live an imitation of somebody else's life with perfection." From "The Bhagavad Gita," one of the ancient holy scriptures of Hinduism (2nd century BCE).*

If we want to break boundaries of thought, creativity and science, we must then create a work environment that will influence our thoughts freely. Free of dogma, free of thought limitations, free of compartmentalization, free of putting every topic in "its drawer."

Physical untidiness (the kind that is under control) will promise us countless options of creating and different combinations. Our fertile mind will be inspired from the countless stimuli around us, without us limiting them in the drawers of our minds.

*The great artist Pablo Picasso said: "Every child is an artist. The problem is how to remain an artist once we grow up."*

\*\*\*

From now on, do not be angry with your children if their rooms are not completely tidy. Tell yourselves repeatedly that the sense of freedom will allow them to utilize their intellectual and creative abilities in all areas of creation and thought.

# SECTION 3

LOVING OURSELVES AND ENJOYING OUR LIVES

# CHAPTER 16

# Love Thyself

**Let's be honest: More than a few of us are our own worst enemies—with our constant judgment, constant criticism, guilt feelings, pangs-of-conscience, self-flagellation, lack of confidence, the comparisons we make with others, and many other ways. How to treat this? Here are some excellent tips:**

- From this very moment, let's begin loving ourselves. From now on, it doesn't matter at all what others say about you, what matters is what you say about yourself.
- Know this: the way we treat ourselves will be reflected in the way others will treat us. And so, begin at once to treat yourselves with respect and appreciation. It will come back to you.
- Never compare your accomplishments to the accomplishments of others. Compare them only to your starting point in life.
- Amplify your successes and minimize your failures. Live with a sense of fullness and not lack.
- Be forgiving of others, but firstly of yourselves.
- Do not act out of a sense of victimhood in life, but out of a sense of control in it. And if you still feel like a victim, know that you are a victim only of yourself, your actions and conduct. This is true for nations and countries as well.

- Choose not to pity yourselves, but to believe in yourselves.
- If you have reached a crisis point, hold onto even the smallest positive thing, even a thread. Amplify it, and you will move forward from there.
- Never agree to be the ones who clean up somebody else's mess.
- Know that there is always a new way of dealing with difficulties and challenges, a way that you haven't yet tried.
- Never, under any circumstance, give up your sense of self. Do not disregard your emotional and intellectual needs for the sake of anybody else's needs, even your loved ones.
- And always remember: One cannot love others if they are disconnected from themselves.

*Ralph Waldo Emerson, the American philosopher and poet, said: "What lies behind you and what lies in front of you, pales in comparison to what lies inside of you."*

*The great Roman poet Horace said: "Adversity reveals genius, prosperity conceals it." Meaning, failures and challenges force us to discover within us creative solutions that we would have never otherwise thought of if we weren't in a state of crisis.*

*The author J.K Rowling, who wrote the successful book series "Harry Potter," spoke at the commencement address at Harvard and said: "It is impossible to live without failing at something, unless you live so cautiously that you might as well not have lived at all—in which case, you fail by default. Failure gave me an inner security that I had never attained by passing examinations. Failure taught me things about myself that I could have learned no other way. So, given a Time Turner, I would tell my twenty-one-year-old self that personal happiness lies in knowing that life is not a check-list of acquisition or achievement. Your qualifications, your CV, are not your life, though you will meet many people of my age and older who confuse the two. Life is difficult, and complicated, and beyond anyone's total control, and the humility to know that will enable you to survive its vicissitudes."*

\*\*\*

And most importantly: Know that all the talents and abilities you were blessed with are not meant to inflate your ego and glorify your name and honor, but to contribute to society. Otherwise, they have no real value. And so, share your light and abilities with others. Do it with love because that is your mission and calling in life.

# CHAPTER 17

## Let's Forgive Ourselves

**Many of us, who experience the daily difficulties and frustrations of life, often feel that we are sailing alone in the boat of life, which is struggling in the stormy waters and high waves. Also, in our personal lives we feel similarly—as if the difficulties are ours alone. From our outside perspective it seems to us that the lives of those around us are calm, easier, powerful and self-fulfilling.**

Well, the opposite is true. Few people experience satisfaction, success and self-fulfillment on a daily basis. Even celebrities and successful people, whose achievements cannot be denied, testify that they often feel the sense of failure, missing out and lack of contentment. Almost all of them can attest to the bumpy road on the way to the top. Many of them become addicted to drugs, alcohol and dangerous hobbies as an escape from frustration.

It is important that we know that there are no shortcuts in life. The road to success is paved with struggles, difficulties and challenges, and don't believe anyone who says otherwise. Winston Churchill, the great former leader of Britain, said about this: *"Success is all about going from failure to failure without losing enthusiasm."*

From this we see that the sense of failure that we often feel due to problems or difficulties is completely subjective and often has no connection to reality whatsoever. However, it is important that we understand that it determines our quality of life, and usually not for the better.

If we learn to love ourselves with our weaknesses, frustrations, disappointments, failures, stupid slips of tongue and foolish actions—the better off we will be. If we learn to love all these and forgive ourselves, our quality of life will be infinitely better.

*The Dalai Lama put it this way: "If you don't love yourself, you cannot love others. You will not be able to love others. If you have no compassion for yourself then you are not able of developing compassion for others."*

The day that we stop thinking that all our actions are measured, weighed, and constantly receive a passing or failing grade, we will feel immense relief and freedom. When we understand that we are, and we alone are our only critics, and that only we have the right to criticize ourselves, then we will feel happy. By the same token, we must internalize that we have no right to judge others. We lack the ability and legitimacy to do so.

*Lao Tzu, one of the great Chinese philosophers, said: "Because one believes in oneself, one doesn't try to convince others. Because one is content with oneself, one doesn't need others' approval. Because one accepts oneself, the whole world accepts him or her."*

The most important thing in life is that we are full of love and compassion. First of all, for ourselves, and then for our surroundings. A person who is disconnected from themselves cannot love others, and that is why it is not selfishness but a basic need.

So, let's throw away the tabs we've been keeping and be forgiving toward ourselves, our friends, our family members and the people around us.

*Jack Kornfield, the American psychologist, author and Buddhist, said: "If your compassion does not include yourself, it is incomplete."*

# CHAPTER 18

# Leaving Behind Obligations of the Past

**In my childhood neighborhood of Maoz Aviv, the local grocery store owner used to have a black notepad where he wrote down his clients' tabs. I remember the notepad as a threatening sword, as an emotional burden that haunted my parents and left us constantly with the feeling of obligation, of unpaid debt, of an old account that must be continuously checked. The feeling of unfinished business.**

This black notepad is a metaphor: it's like a little demon inside us reminding us all the time that we have unfinished business. Instead of dealing with him, decide to live without him. Throw away the pen and forget yesterday's offense. When you're feeling hurt, respond immediately in a straightforward manner and close the subject. This will allow you to go on with your life without carrying the pain and the feeling that "I have to pay this person back for what they said or did." If you haven't responded right away, do not prolong the matter and let out what is on your chest.

People who keep in their hearts and minds the "debt" of those around them, the insults, the fury and anger, cannot be happy. The feelings of insult manage them. They are not available for renewal and growth.

Their consciousness, thoughts and spirits are busy with that insult, and this feeling prevents them from moving toward new objectives. They are frustrated, bitter and angry, their channels of energy and rejuvenation are blocked, and are bound to burst in the least convenient situation, with the result being a big fight and a drawn-out burden.

*Nelson Mandela, anti-apartheid revolutionary and former president of South Africa, said about this: "Resentment is like drinking poison and then hoping it will kill your enemies."*

*The Chinese philosopher Lao Tzu, father of Taoism, said: "Stiffness is a companion of death. Flexibility a companion of life."*

As a rule, control in life is controlling our anger and the way we resolve painful topics with the people in our lives, both personally and professionally. If we control the process, set the time for a conversation and decide the main points, we can be focused on the target, reach effective results and gain cooperation.

Another point to think about: it's important not to settle a score and not to get aggravated over every little thing, but to have a confrontation only over substantial matters. Even if we are right, we'd better be smart and properly consider if it's worth going to war over a trivial and unimportant matter.

And not merely that, it's best if we generally ignore and slide over the problem, get over things and let them flow in the stream of life. Luckily, the stream of life allows us all to make changes and turns. Usually, we will discover sometime later that we've forgotten the whole event and don't understand what we were even mad about.

A reaction, therefore, is recommended within a very short time period, and even then, only if the matter is fundamental. How do we do this? Very simply: we wait several seconds to formulate our thoughts and feelings. It is the nature of a stone that is thrown into water to create bigger and bigger circles. Sometimes it's just best not to throw the stone and let things pass.

And what of the most important type of forgiveness in life, forgiveness of ourselves? Every person acts from a unique system of feelings, expectations, prior experiences from childhood and our education, qualities and the structure of our personality. Let's forgive ourselves for the mistakes we make and have made in our lives. Let's embrace ourselves in any situation, in our successes and failures, since it is our natural right as human beings to make mistakes. It's important that we know: there is almost nothing that cannot be mended.

*Also about this, the smart philosopher Lau Tzu said: "When you are content to be simply yourself and don't compare or compete, everybody will respect you."*

This does not mean that we must give up the will to grow, evolve and improve. In fact, it is improvement and constant evolving that are the key to our personal growth. We will always aspire to do things better than we have in the past, set a higher standard for ourselves each time anew, and yet, we must learn to be forgiving of our weaknesses, our dwindling emotional and physical abilities, our fatigue, our forgetfulness, our stresses and burdens.

\*\*\*

Let's love ourselves as we are. That is the whole philosophy in a nutshell. In addition, let's love the environment we live in as it is. Let's find the advantages in every situation and every reality, amplify them and enjoy them to the fullest.

# CHAPTER 19

# Why Suffer?!

**A person comes into the world for a measured and limited amount of time, and so there is no point for them to suffer in life. The highest value in life should be pleasure—a person must enjoy every single moment of their lives: Enjoy the flowers' blossoming, the sunrise, the universe, their loved ones, their friends, their children, spending time with people and with themselves, all the while, contributing their abilities and talents to their surroundings and feeling content for doing so.**

*Marcus Aurelius, the Roman emperor and philosopher, said: "It is not death that a man should fear, but he should fear never beginning to live."*

And yet, many people feel guilty when they enjoy themselves. Others feel uncomfortable about the abundance and wealth that surrounds them, making them feel the need to apologize. Oftentimes, this is the result of education and messages they received in childhood, which claimed that enjoyment is illegitimate. According to these messages, we are obligated to tasks and mission that must be carried out, and satisfying our own needs is considered selfish and therefore negative. Suffering is the so-called price we must pay for receiving the gift of life.

Here is the place to add, in parentheses, that in the State of Israel there is an added dimension—the memory of The Holocaust. Many of the founders of the state were Holocaust survivors who found it hard to be joyful. In spite of trying their best to give their children normal lives, they subconsciously communicated to them distress and pain, and so their children later also found it hard to be joyous and to adopt an optimistic outlook on life.

The French philosopher of the renaissance period, Michel de Montaigne, claimed that man himself is responsible for his suffering in the statement: "No one suffers for very long but by their own fault."

It is not necessary for life to be full of suffering or difficulties in order to get results. Where has this myth come from? Under no circumstances should you pass on this erroneous thinking to your children. Do not make them feel, through overt or hidden messages, guilty about the fact that they seek "the good life." Instead, encourage them to listen to themselves and to experience a life of joy and pleasure.

Serve as an example for them, show them that hard work and investing effort in their personal and professional areas in life do not involve suffering. Moreover, teach them that even if life consists of difficulties, challenges and tasks that are hard and full of effort, this does not mean that all these will turn into a life of suffering, but a life full of challenges and personal contentment, instead.

From this moment on, start thinking differently. Believe wholeheartedly that you are worthy of, and that you earned, your leisure time, fun, pleasure, indulgence and the material and emotional assets in your life. You have no obligation, even in the slightest, to pay anything for your pleasures. Even if you grew up as a child in a poor home or had a tough life that lacked love and human warmth—especially because of this, it is your right to enjoy a life that is rich with the material and spiritual. From this moment on, let go completely of suffering in your life. Choose to live a life of joy and pleasure.

*The author and spiritual guide Byron Katie, claims that emotional distress is the result of people being unsatisfied with their lives: "If you argue against reality you will suffer."*

\*\*\*

And yet, with everything that's been said, it is important never to ignore the suffering of others. Be attentive and empathetic and show social solidarity toward the weak members of society who need assistance. Try your best to donate your time and effort to those who need you, from a standpoint of human dignity and at eye level.

# CHAPTER 20

## Slivers of Happiness

**I watched an American TV show about channeling spirits of people who passed away, and it got me thinking. You can argue about the subject, it's appropriateness, credibility, how scientific it is (or how illusory it is), but there are messages that you cannot argue with. I would like to call attention to the messages that the deceased have sent from "there."**

The spirits of the deceased who "participated" in the show, told the host about very routine things: a dish they used to love, a trip they went on, renovations in their home, a lost wedding ring, a visit to the theater that stuck out in their memory, and so on and so forth. I was astonished by the contrast between "the great story," the "wow" of the channeling itself that the family was so excited about, and the content that the spirits wanted to relay—nothing but "small," esoteric content. They relayed memories/experiences of supposedly little activities, routine-everyday things, which to the outside observer may seem no more meaningful than a feather. And yet, you cannot dispute the fact that these are the events they chose to talk about. That's what has been imprinted on their souls and inner experiences, and that's how they chose to define their lives.

The essence of our lives is made up of the supposedly insignificant little activities. These are the puzzle pieces that make up our lives. The small excitements that a person experiences in their everyday, routine and mundane life, is essentially what determines the quality of their life.

And so, it is best not to wait for life's most exciting moments, for that big trip to New Zealand we've been dreaming about, or for seeing the beautiful nature of the island of Patagonia. We must increase the little pleasures of life right here and now, and increase expressions of love and attention toward our loved ones. The small experiences of life may paint our routine, dull lives in bright colors, and if we increase our small pleasures, these bright colors will not dissipate or fade. We will make sure to repaint it again and again.

Let me share something personal: I habitually start each day at the beach. I leave early, usually at sunrise, and on the way I listen to happy songs that I hum to myself while lightly running on the beach. This encounter with the cool wind, the light run or walk, and the wonderful feeling of the cool waters, recharges me every day with new energy and joy.

***

I recommend that everybody start their day with an activity that will rejuvenate their vitality and energy and give them the strength to live life with pleasure and fun.

# SECTION 4

## THE COLOR OF OUR GLASSES

# CHAPTER 21

# Reflection

**The way in which we interpret our reality, alongside the meaning and context we give to passing events, determines our feelings and thoughts, and as a result, the quality of our lives.**

Oftentimes, when I arrive at a new and unfamiliar place, I look curiously at the faces of the strangers around me and try to figure out their qualities and who they are inside. I observe how they dress, try to decipher their facial expressions, their smiles and the way they look at their surroundings and communicate with others.

I notice how the challenges of life have etched lines of fatigue and exhaustion on the faces of those around me. Too many people are "surviving life" instead of living it. The endless chores of life wear down and eat away at a person's feelings of vitality, fun and basic 'joie de vivre.' They are frequently troubled by issues of finance, health, career and everyday routine troubles, all which prevent them from enjoying life and all its beauty.

During my work of many years with teenagers, I was amazed each time anew by their endless joy of life, creativity, emotional strength, excitement and basic happiness. In my heart, I wondered: At what point along the way do adults lose this? Is the burden of a mortgage to blame? Or is it the exhausting daily work routine? Demanding children? Aging parents? The difficulties in relationships with family, at our workplace, bureaucracy related difficulties, financial stresses and countless other stresses in our lives?

Obviously all these reasons are true, and there are many more reasons that shape our adult lives, but the result is the same. Many of us, at some point in our lives, become adults who are tired, drained and lacking excitement. The kind who've lost that spark in their eyes.

I will transition for a moment from the personal arena to the scientific arena to demonstrate this idea: In historical research, the common thought is that there is no one historical "truth," but historical "stories" (narratives) that are told from different points of view. History, like science, seeks to attribute interpretations for a series of events and facts, and so a hegemonic, collective and dominant story is created (the mainstream). Alongside this, stories of marginal groups develop as well, which give critical interpretations to the hegemonic story and destabilize its "truths" and fundamental assertions. Groups such as minorities, women, homosexuals and marginal social groups, undermine the dominant story and add additional "players" into the ring (facts, statuses and people), who were silenced, suppressed, and pushed to the political and social sidelines of the narrative.

This knowledge that the reality of our lives is not objective but subjective, that this reality is experienced by us from our own points of view, and that each person can interpret it differently or even contrarily—is a very important and significant matter.

For example, the way in which we deal with our failures: There are people who see every failure as another nail in their closet of horrible defeats. Failure will sour their moods, depress them and harm their self-confidence and self-image. This is in comparison to an optimistic person, who will see failure only as a mishap. Moreover, they will learn the lesson through analysis and by drawing conclusions. They will turn the failure into a challenge and opportunity to do something differently and creatively. They will, of course, say to themselves: "If I don't make mistakes or fail during life, it means that I haven't done enough." The optimistic person will always see beyond the momentary failure.

*Wayne Dyer, the American philosopher and author, once said: "When you change the way you look at things, the things you look at change." (https://www.drwaynedyer.com/video/).*

*Thomas Edison said about this: "Many Of Life's Failures Are People Who Did Not Realize How Close They Were to Success When They Gave Up."*

Never let failure cause you to give up. Failure and difficulty are an important and basic stage in the process of growth, progress, professionalization, and constant improvement in life, in every area.

Do not let feelings of guilt control you. Many people live with the constant feeling of guilt. This is the result of education and social conventions that set a constant bar for us and so-called "proper" rules of conduct. We all operate under human, cultural, and social codes in our different life circles. Many of us feel that we don't **hold up** to the criteria required of us socially, financially and professionally.

The moment we shed these conventions and operate according to our conscience, our hearts and inner truth, it will be easier for us to act in the different areas of our lives, and we will also succeed on the professional and personal paths we choose. Many people judge themselves and their friends according to "the standard of life:" How to behave, what one should say and in which situation, etc.. Once we understand that this standard is a figment of our imaginations, and we are not obligated to anything but our happiness and inner truth alone, it is as if we shed this cloak that was burdening and weighing heavily on our lives. Many people would discover that their human conscience and intuition is infinitely better than any social norm. The moment we stop worrying about being different and unique, we will find our happiness.

If we pause several times a day from the race of our lives and look around, we will discover that happiness is right around the corner.

The change in your life will begin once you tell yourself that what really matters is your sense of happiness and freedom. Start loving yourselves in this very moment. Put yourself—your emotional welfare and your health—in first place, before all the other tasks in your life. This will simplify your lives immensely, make them more pleasant, and will immediately stop your crazy race of trying to please your surroundings. This is not selfishness, but a necessity of the demanding world we live in so that we may take care of our physical and emotional health. People who do not love themselves, cannot love others, and the quality of their lives will be terrible.

\*\*\*

Remember all the while: the price of silencing your inner voice is infinitely greater than the social and economical benefits of silencing it. It's a price of harming one's emotional and physical health to the point of destruction. Listen to your inner voice and do not be afraid to act on it and express it in the public sphere. Your authentic voice is essentially how you express your existence in the universe.

## CHAPTER 22

# Minimize Difficulties and They Really Will Shrink

**Here is the key sentence for life: Our attitude toward difficulties, challenges and tasks in our lives is what determines how much space they take up from our emotional energy, thoughts and worries. If we amplify the difficulties in our lives, they will grow too much grander proportions than what they really are. If we treat them lightly, they will be light.**

Easier said than done, but this is the challenge of our complex, 21st century lives. If we don't treat life with ease, our lives will free as though we're constantly swimming upstream. A subjective view of life is what determines how the body and mind respond to difficulties, pressures and effort. Meaning, it is a choice.

The body responds directly to the mind. It notices our stress and warning signs, vigilance, fear and tension. We all wear down the power of our bodies and weaken its energy and our life fuse.

*We better adopt the famous statement of Winston Churchill, Former Prime Minister of Britain: "The pessimist sees difficulty in every opportunity, the optimist sees the opportunity in every difficulty."*

This is the essence of life on earth: it is made of thousands of puzzle pieces, some of which we will have a hard time piecing together in the picture of our lives, and will try to get rid of. But without them, the picture will be incomplete. Life cannot only consist of easy tasks. If so—starting today—let us accept with love and understanding the different setbacks in our lives, the small mishaps and the occasional tiresome routine. Let's change our terminology and see these difficulties as challenges, as tests we must pass. These are essential hurdles, which strengthen our ability to cope, our resilience, our patience and our human endurance. It is a process of ongoing learning. It is how we grow.

*Greg Anderson, former US basketball player, said: "Focus on the journey, not the destination. Joy is found not in finishing an activity but in doing it."*

Recently, we went through the exhausting process of moving homes. There are not enough words to describe the setbacks, countless mishaps and disappointments we encountered along the way. But the moment we decided to accept everything with love, the process became more tolerable and less aggravating. I won't lie, sometimes we had to remind ourselves not to get angry, that this was the price we had to pay for the apartment of our dreams. That said, the process was infinitely easier thanks to the decision we made to treat the matter with forgiveness and patience. And indeed, this patience paid off.

This story brings me to the topic of shortcuts in life. The long road we take in order to reach our goals in life—personal, professional and familial goals— is always paved with great effort and by recruiting our mental, physical and financial powers. And yet, there is no other way. Achievements always come as a result of deep digging, great effort and investment, and this is the lesson we must give our children.

Thomas Alva Edison, who registered a record number of patents in the world (1,093!) and whose light bulb invention is considered his greatest accomplishment, once said: *"I've not failed, I've just found 10,000 ways that don't work. Every failed attempt is another step forward."* And he knew what he was talking about. He carried out over 1000 failed attempts in order to reach the functioning light bulb, however, he did not see it as a failure, but an experiment, a way of learning in order to reach a better result in the future.

Would you like some encouraging examples? Here:

- Albert Einstein, one of the greatest physicists of all times and father of the Theory of Relativity, had a difficult time learning, speaking and writing. He finished his studies with relatively low grades and had a hard time finding a job. While working as an examiner at a patent office in Bern, he dedicated much of his time to research in physics, which turned into four famous articles that were published in 1905 and that subsequently changed physics and the way we understand the world.

- The writer J.K Rowling spent six years writing the first "Harry Potter" book, and was supported by welfare during those years. She proposed her book to twelve book publishers and was rejected by them all, until she finally managed to publish the book and the rest is history.

- Oprah Winfrey, the famous TV host, was born to impoverished parents in the state of Mississippi, she then grew up in several foster homes. Later on, she arrived at a boarding school that she also had to leave due to lack of beds. At 19, she began reporting on a local Tennessee news channel, and from there her career as a journalist and actress took off.

No doubt all these examples feature people with innate talent. However, without the effort and determination to achieve their goals, they never would have reached the top.

\*\*\*

Let's remember: the ability to invest effort and deal with countless disappointments and failures (which should be called unsuccessful experiments) on the way, is what will lead us to achieving the goals that we set. Our feelings of capability and our willingness to invest are the deciding factors.

# CHAPTER 23

## So Lucky it Didn't Work Out

**How much anguish do we all feel because of our failures? We are interested in getting a position, and our superiors choose someone else. We plan a trip, and for unexpected reasons we have to cancel it. We are about to begin a course, but it's canceled suddenly due to lack of participants. We would like to be set up with someone, but they, much to our chagrin, are not interested. How many of us haven't sometimes felt as though everything is hard for us, and for others, things flow so easily?**

Pause. Take a break. I suggest we look at things differently. Actually, not differently—inversely.

If something "doesn't work out for us," it means that our purpose doesn't lie there, and neither does our desired success. Our purpose in the universe and the optimal self-fulfillment of our personalities and souls—is elsewhere. The universe saves us from wasting energy in a place that isn't suitable for us and where we will be unsuccessful. If we haven't managed to arrange a meeting with someone for technical reasons, there are cosmic reasons for this. The meeting was not meant to take place, at least not in the timing we wanted. How many times in life have we said to ourselves, "I'm so lucky I didn't go," "I'm so lucky it didn't work out," "I'm so lucky I didn't stick to the original plan," because the opportunity that followed was a thousand times better.

Even so-called esoteric events are not coincidental. If I wasn't able to reach someone by phone, there is probably a reason for it. It is possible that I'm not even meant to contact them, and maybe another time I will achieve better results than if I were to speak to them now. Maybe, in this moment, they are not emotionally available to speak to me and respond to my needs, and the fact that they are not available to me now saves me from distress and suffering.

***

Let's begin thinking in this way about things and we will be spared the anguish of "missing out." The meaning of this is that our fortune is elsewhere.

# CHAPTER 24

# The Glass Half Full

**Our sages have said "Who is rich? One who is satisfied with his lot," and indeed, the feeling of satisfaction in our lives isn't related to our bank account, nor to the size of the apartment we live in, and it is not measured with quantitative measures. What really matters is how we feel about our lives, our own selves, and situation, and how happy we are with what we have in life.**

Studies show that there is no connection between a person's financial situation and their levels of happiness. What matters is that we feel "rich." According to our definition "a sense and awareness of fullness" means that every day we feel that our lives are rich with "assets," we feel that we are living with an abundance of "gifts," and living in the frequency and awareness of "I have." All these are not obvious things.

The phrase "I have" refers to all the emotional, spiritual and material "assets" that we were blessed with in our lives—our humane and professional skills, freedom, health, our dear family, our beloved friends, our hobbies, the roof over our heads, the food on our tables, the education we acquired, our workplace, the beauty of nature around us, the wonderful music that uplifts our spirits, art, literature and everything else the universe has to offer.

Let us then change in this very moment the way we think about life. Let us be grateful for it and amplify in our consciousness all the "gifts" we have.

*The Roman emperor Marcus Aurelius said: "Think of what you have rather than of what you lack. Of the things you have, select the best and then reflect how eagerly you would have sought them if you did not have them."*

The joy and appreciation for the gifts in our lives will attract more gifts to us: prolific and blessed work, happy occasions, people with good energy, growth and development in all areas, empowering and uplifting experiences and good energy that affects our lives and the lives of our loved ones.

The sense and awareness of fullness will bring forth the fullness and abundance in reality. Living with the sense of fullness will attract into your reality a life full of joy, financial assets, creativity, growth, professional and spiritual development and emotional assets.

On the other hand, in accordance with the rule that "like attracts like," the sense of constant lack and focusing on what isn't rather than what is, will turn our lives into lives of lack, the kind characterized by constant scarcity of not merely finances, but of joy and experiences of progress and growth. In this kind of life, the constant feeling of "stuckness" will prevail—financially, socially, professionally and spiritually—and culminate with lack of advancement in every area.

In order to create a positive reality for our lives, we must think positively and optimistically, in a way that will deeply convince us that "everything is Okay" and that what we plan for our lives will succeed.

A positive reality cannot exist with negative thinking behind it. The negative thinking will sabotage the positive reality that we want to create for ourselves. A strong belief that we have the power to advance ourselves and our lives in the direction that we want must also be added.

With that, we must also know and understand that the challenges we face are, in fact, the essence of our lives on earth. Life cannot only consist of simple and easy tasks. And so, from now on, let us accept as natural and obvious the various setbacks in our lives, the small and big mishaps and the failures. Let us change our terminology: instead of frustration or anger, let us see these difficulties as challenges on the way to the targets that we set for ourselves.

This is a process of ongoing learning. Remember, there are no shortcuts in life. Achievements and successes always come as a result of deep digging, great effort and investment.

*Bill Porter is an American born with cerebral palsy. He wanted with all his heart to be a salesman, but there wasn't a single company that would hire him. At some point, Porter offered a company in Oregon to give him the hardest area for sales. The company had nothing to lose, they agreed, and very quickly, Porter became the most successful salesman in the district at selling medications, baking products and house-ware products. Porter worked at the same company for over forty years, and in 1995 a series of articles was published about him in a local paper. There wasn't a single person in Oregon that didn't know his name. His inspiring story became a documentary film in 2002, and since then, until today, it is an inspiration for many people thanks to his willpower, determination and optimism. This story exemplifies that even when a person is at a low point physically, health-wise, financially or socially, they are still able to reach the top thanks to willpower, effort and determination.*

*The successful English actor Robert Collier said: "Success is the sum of small efforts, repeated day in and day out."*

\*\*\*

If you wish to create a new reality for yourselves, use this power of yours. Believe that you are capable of achieving the goal you set for yourself, show determination, faith and persistence, and head on your way.

# CHAPTER 25

# The Choice to be Happy

**When we emerged from our mother's womb, breathing air into our lungs for the first time, we did not know what awaited for us here on this earth. As we matured, we understood that these precious years, which are a gift from God, have been given to us for a limited time only; every person according to what God and the universe allotted them.**

Our lives stretch from point to point, from the beginning to the end. They are part of the enormous movement of the universe that flows forward and sweeps along with it all living creatures and everything that is in existence on the planet. During this lifetime, we are given the option to live our lives with free will: will we choose the path of honesty and decency, or the opposite? Will we choose to bring light unto our surroundings or the opposite?

Also the question of whether or not we choose to be happy, is in our hands. The measure of human happiness is determined by the person's feeling and not external elements. It is a personal, subjective statement, as was said by *Abraham Lincoln, former US president: "Most folks are about as happy as they make up their minds to be."*

- A person who chooses to be happy will try and find the good in everything. They will try not to intensify their difficulties, but the opposite. They will try to overcome their ego for the good of marital harmony, peace between neighbors or colleagues and a more pleasant living environment. They will learn to make the distinction between standing up for their values and principles, and protecting their "honor," or, in other words: their ego.

- A person who chooses to be happy will learn to look around them and enjoy the little and supposed insignificant things in life. They will derive pleasure from the fragrance of a lemon tree in spring, from the blooming of a tiny flower in the garden. They will immensely enjoy the taste of freshly squeezed carrot juice at the local market, and will watch the waves of the ocean with concentration and emotional connection.

- A person who chooses to be happy will be forgiving of themselves, their partner, their family, their colleagues or their friends. They will "cancel" difficulties and problems—not out of lack of responsibility, but out of the realization that anger, resentment and negative energy are simply unnecessary. This inner insight, that anger and tension muddies the atmosphere and is a burden on life, will necessarily lead them to be conciliatory toward their surroundings.

- A person who chooses to be happy will learn to live according to their truth, but at the same time will be considerate of others' feelings. Their conscience will be clean, they will live with the sense of wholeness and fulfillment of their desires, and will not live their life in reaction to the actions of others or out of the need to explain their actions. They will have the emotional resilience to stand up to social criticism and not fold when faced with the pressures around them. They will stick to their truth and principles, all while being loyal to themselves, their emotions, their needs, and most importantly—their conscience.

*"Optimism, a smile, and hope. What little we need for life to be happy, and it is all within us and our way of thinking." So stated the Roman emperor and philosopher Marcus Aurelius.*

*John Lennon once shared: "When I was 5 years old, my mother always told me that happiness was the key to life. When I went to school, they asked me what I wanted to be when I grew up. I wrote down 'happy'. They told me I didn't understand the assignment, and I told them they didn't understand life."*

*Buddha said: "Praise and blame, gain and loss, pleasure and sorrow come and go like the wind. To be happy, rest like a giant tree in the midst of them all."*

\*\*\*

An optimistic viewpoint and the understanding that difficulties are an inseparable part of life will lead us to the understanding that, in the end, the difficulties pass and we are capable of dealing with them.

# CHAPTER 26

# Turning the Lemons into Lemonade

**The easiest and most common way to deal with hard situations is to complain, to go into a state of despondency, depression, despair and defeatism. Many people blame others for the situations they are in and get comfortable in their victimhood. However, there is another option: instead of sinking into the feeling that there is no way out, we can make the best out of the situation. We can decide to fight and not give up under any circumstance.**

*The Spanish writer Miguel de Cervantes said the following: "Every man is the sum of his own works."*

After we make this decision, we may discover within us an inner strength, courage, and will to attack our goal. Suddenly we will discover as if another being, supposedly a foreign one, operating from within us, strengthening us and giving us joy and the sense of rejuvenation. We will discover that when we are full of optimism, our surroundings will become full of joy and confidence about the future.

Oftentimes, it is actually our difficulties and challenges that bear our next successes. Challenges force us to try harder and be creative.

They bring us to places we never thought we would reach if not for the need to find creative solutions and step outside the box.

*Evgeny Smirnov was a world renown break dancer who won more than thirty medals in dance competitions. In 2012, he was involved in a car accident, which resulted in him losing one of his legs. It seemed as though his dance career should have been over, but Smirnov did not give up. He stuck with his love of dance, and with great effort continued dancing with just one leg in the unique and phenomenal way that is typical of him. This example shows that with willpower and determination, one can overcome great obstacles.*

It's true, our optimism is usually not based in reality. At least not at first. But it doesn't matter. We can change reality. The moment we make the internal decision about it, we're already halfway there.

As a rule, optimism does not depend at all on reality. It is a way of thinking, self-persuasion and adopting a positive standpoint about life. Thinking positively makes a person act and create based on the supposition that they can change reality (for the better, of course). If a person conveys to their environment that they are determined to solve their difficulties and problems, the others will tend to follow and believe in them. And with that, we've already passed the halfway point.

The thing that blocks people from solving problems and difficulties is a psychological block. People refuse to believe that it is in their power to move the cart of their life and pull it out of the mud. They calculate what is to come in their minds, usually in a pessimistic way, which intensifies the difficulties—and that's how they pile up imaginary blocks and obstacles on the way to solving the problem.

*Canadian Senator Douglas Donald Everett said: "There are some people who live in a dream world and some who face reality; and then there are those who turn one into the other."*

*And Stephen Hawking, the English Astrophysicist who became sick with ALS and managed, over the course of five decades, to do research and become a cultural icon, said: "However difficult life may seem, there is always something you can do and succeed at."*

\*\*\*

We must change our negative way of thinking and imagine ourselves overcoming our difficulties and "turning the lemon into lemonade." And then, the psychological block and the "fear of doing" will be released. We have already stated: a large part of the change occurs in the mind and every great creation starts with a dream, sometimes even an imaginary and completely unrealistic one.

# SECTION 5

## US AND OUR SURROUNDINGS

# CHAPTER 27

## See Others at Eye Level

**Who among us hasn't ever fallen in the trap of arrogance and feeling superior to others? It is a very natural thing. The subjective feeling that I am better than someone else, that I know it all, that I am smarter, more successful and more talented than others, causes us to fail in life.**

*The Politician, scientist and writer, Benjamin Franklin said: "As pride increases, fortune declines." and Harry Truman, former US president said: "It is amazing what you can accomplish if you do not care who gets the credit."*

Let's try and change our thinking and see ourselves as completely equal to other people. Let's listen to them, respect them, and understand that, to them, their lives are holy and important, just as our lives are holy and important to us.

*Nachmanides, the medieval Jewish scholar, wrote of the importance of humility in his famous letter to his son: "Speak calmly at all times, and avoid anger, act humbly and modestly before everyone and consider everyone as greater than yourself."*

Every person is a whole world of their own. Every person is the expression of the universe and manifestation of the divine essence on the planet. That is why we are commanded to respect every person, no matter who they are; rich or poor, pretty or ugly, important or a commoner, tall or short, young or old, regardless of religion, race or gender. We must respect everyone as human-beings.

*Rabbi Israel Salanter, founder of the ethics movement in Judaism, said: "When I see a prideful person, I feel nauseated."*

We must see people at eye level. We mustn't be condescending but nor should we humiliate ourselves in the face of authority, power, money, status and the like. We must stand up for our human dignity and not let others hurt us. At the same time, we must not trample the human dignity of another, even when we are sure they deserve it. Even if we hold a position of power, we must not forget that just like we got this position, we can easily lose it as well.

Position, money, social and economic status, rank—all these do not give us our human dignity. This dignity is given to us as a privilege, the moment we are born as human-beings. But we can strengthen our standing by contributing to others, by doing good deeds, by acting gracefully and kindly to those in need, by acting with honesty, decency, with wisdom and according to moral judgment.

Many times in my life, I found myself judging the people around me. My family, my friends, my students, my neighbors, my superiors, people I liked a lot and people I did not like so much. I found faults in their behavior, their actions or lack thereof, their words, their way of life and a thousand other topics. I reached the conclusion (which

I repeat to myself over and over again so I don't mindlessly stumble into this trap) that this is unacceptable behavior for a few reasons:

Being in the position that always judges others, means placing yourself morally, mentally and humanly above others. Based on what? On what basis are we allowed to judge others?

Here are some reasons why we must not do this:

- As humans, we are on the exact same level as other humans. We all have qualities that have been given to us by God, we were all blessed with life, we all face reality according to our abilities, understanding, consciousness, and physical, mental and financial abilities.

- And who decided that what we think is right, is the "absolute truth?" And that there even is an absolute truth? What's true will always be our opinion, based on the glasses we wear, our value system, the norms and social codes of our society, which are completely subjective.

- Our sages have said: *"Do not judge your fellow man until you have reached his place." Meaning, from where we stand, we do not have the ability to judge the actions of another person who is in another place, under different conditions, and different circumstances. Under those circumstances, the person acted according to their own judgment, feelings, spiritual needs, fears, sensations, memories, and according to the interpretation they gave to the reality they were experiencing. And because the interpretation is completely subjective, we have no right to judge or criticize them.*

- *And another reason why we do not have the right to judge others is because we are commanded to be tolerant. We must accept it as a given that the other person is different from us, that they think differently, act differently, and that their value system will be different. This is the most natural state, and is a result of the diversity that is typical of us and our differences as human beings. If we were all similar, then where would be all the beauty of human creativity, variety of opinions, pluralism of ideas, the genius, the science, the abundance of human creation in different fields? That is the magic of human existence: the countless human shades of character, beauty, culture, thought, food, dress, and all other areas of life.*

We must encourage originality, creativity, different ways of thinking, and heterogeneity. This is the dimension that enriches our lives, diversifies us and prevents us from living in a monotone, boring world. This is the vitality of our lives, which enriches our existence in this universe with a million shades. This is our human contribution to this wonderful world. Let us not suppress this creativity. Let us accept others as our equals, and leave behind the metaphorical seat of judgment we sit in.

*The 19th century author Isaac Leib Peretz wrote: "No two trees are the same, no two leaves are the same, and certainly no two humans are the same."*

*Meaning that no two people are alike. Everyone is equal as far as human rights, but different in their qualities and talents.*

***

*There is only one instance when we are commanded to judge and stop other people's actions. In the case of immoral and inhumane behavior that harms other people, be it emotionally, financially, physically or in any other way. Then we must do everything we can, as private people and as nations, in order to halt these despicable actions.*

# CHAPTER 28

# See Others as People Not Things

**Many of us are unaware that we see other people as functions (tools) and not as human beings. Starting with CEOs who often see their employees as nothing but manpower and judge them by quantitative criterion, or factory managers who judge their workers solely by their output, or teachers who are judged by the percentage of their students who succeed in their final exams.**

*Sometimes, it is the doctor who cannot see the person "behind" the patient, the clerk who gives service to a customer but is blind to their needs and stresses, or the consumers in a supermarket who do not see the exhausted and transparent woman behind the checkout counter. Sometimes it's the army commander who must guide his soldiers to carry out complex missions, or even a loving partner, whose senses have faded after many years of marriage and views the person they live with as someone with a specific role, and they see themselves this way, too.*

*The moment a person stops seeing their fellow man as a human being but sees them only as something that serves a function, this is a serious sign for moral deterioration, emotional exhaustion and fatigue, and the result is a decrease in humane, familial and institutional success and productivity.*

*You cannot succeed in life when you do not see the humanity of the people involved in it. The moment you see only the mission in front of you, and there is no moral, ethical or spiritual character behind it, but only purposefulness, practicality and gain—then you have lost.*

*The Chinese philosopher Lao Tzu said: "He who controls others may be powerful, but he who has mastered himself is mightier still."*

*Even the most successful commercial project must have a moral and ethical foundation.*
*Take for example a phone company that wishes to increase its profits. It is important that even a company like this should operate not only from business motives, but also out of the commitment to connect people. They must see it as socially significant, helpful during an emergency, assisting the communication between people and families and so on. A message such as this, that is conveyed to the company employees, will be an integral part of the sales and marketing of the product, just like the regular maintenance of the technical infrastructure. It will be considered a spiritual goal and a goal of the utmost importance, and therefore the marketers will feel like partners in this mission.*

*A food company that markets a new product, must be open about it having nutritional value that is important for people, contributing to their health, its natural components and so on.*

*When marketing a product, it is important to emphasize its value for the person buying it. A healthy product contributes to quality of life, raises one's standard of living and helps the one using it. Any product when marketed with the correct strategy, can be successful and sell very well.*

*Sometimes I look at couples who have been living together in harmony for many years, and I try and solve the riddle of what holds them together. Over the years, I discovered what they all have in common: they share a spiritual outlook that binds them. They do not build their lives on the material alone, but there is also a spiritual dimension to their relationship. This dimension guarantees their success.*

*I do not mean to claim that spiritual people will not split up, but that their chances of surviving together, smoothing over problems in their relationship, being attentive to each other and aware of themselves and their partners—is what will enable them to have an unconditional relationship, integrity, honesty, transparency, and ultimately the success of their marriage.*

*There are people who claim to love and be attached to their partners. On the other hand, it has been years since they had a heart-to-heart talk with them. How are they connected? Just as I am attached to my old pair of slippers, which I will miss when they are gone, so are they attached to the comfort of their home, and they know they will find it tidy and warm when they arrive. The table, the chairs, the pictures and carpet will be in their places. That is how they see their partners—as an object in their lives. They are not interested in their stresses or their pain. It is enough for them to be by their side as an object, a thing, an accessory. They do not communicate with the soul of their partner, just as they are not in communication with their own. On the contrary, they run from it like from wildfire. They will always find a reason to go and run some errands, go shopping, go for a walk, just so they do not have to look them in the eyes, all so they do not have to be emotionally intimate with their partners or themselves.*

*I tell couples who feel like an object: save your souls. It is infinitely more important than any other physical need. Do not let it die. Look for a mate that can fulfill your emotional needs, as well as the physical. Do not settle in life! If you have reached this point, close your ears to the voices that tell you to stay at all costs.*

\*\*\*

*Do what you feel, and the universe will be with you. Nobody is in your place, or has the ability or the right to judge you. You have the right to be happy. No person is able or permitted to take this privilege from you.*

# CHAPTER 29

## Do Not Use Labels

**Following many years of education and pedagogy work with teenagers, I have reached the conclusion that the key to the development of students depends on their teachers and educators, and the messages they convey regarding their students' ability to succeed.**

*The American psychologist Abraham Maslow, founder of the "humanistic theory" in psychology, said: "What is necessary to change a person is to change his awareness of himself." (Abraham Maslow in a film about self-actualization, 1968, available on YouTube)*

For two years, I taught a small class that was considered to be the "slowest" class in the school. It received the name "the challenging class," and the label "slow" stuck to its students, who believed with all their hearts that they could not succeed. Without thinking about it, subconsciously, the entire teacher staff treated this class very forgivingly, with the sense that there was no point in demanding any effort from its students, since they were simply incapable, since it was a shame to invest in them, because they lacked any learning skills, etc..

As expected, the students of the class finished high school without a diploma, while we, the teacher staff, saw it as a success that we were able to at least keep them "off the streets." We told ourselves that we prevented them from wandering aimlessly, we provided them with an educational and social structure, and that was the most important thing.

Several months after finishing school, I received a phone call from the military asking to interview me about three of the students, who, as it turned out, were in training for very prestigious and responsible jobs in the army. There were only 14 students in the class, and as far as I know, three of them did not enlist (In Israel there is mandatory military service). The three about whom I was contacted, had successfully passed their tests, which testified to the highest of mental and cognitive abilities. In other words, almost a third of all the students who were drafted.

Their results astonished me from every possible angle. I reached the conclusion that all along we were completely mistaken about those "problem" students. Due to problematic behavior that resulted from troubles at home, learning difficulties, concentration problems, and issues with adaptation, we came to the conclusion that the students lacked any learning skills. We put them in a "learning ghetto" in our minds and also physically, and labeled them with a label that they felt obligated to justify. They matched themselves to the messages we were sending out. Both we and they had no expectations and no requirements of them.

This event changed my thinking and awareness. I reached the conclusion that we must treat every person or student as if they have very high abilities. We must speak to them in this way, and convey to them that they have extraordinary abilities, and believe this with all our hearts. If we train ourselves to think this way, we will treat students less forgivingly and require from them effort and meaningful learning. We must make the effort to pique their interests, stimulate them with experiences, stories, and challenges. We must try to find the thread that reaches their hearts and recruit them into action.

I remember well a weaker student in my class, who made a comment relevant to the topic of the lesson. I complimented him that his remark was a testament to his wisdom. It is hard to describe the student's reaction—from that moment on, he sat through the lesson, writing and concentrating. At the end of the class, he picked up all the chairs and informed me that the lesson was great (I remind you, this was a 12th grade history lesson... definitely no picnic).

It is important to emphasize that we, teachers and educators, must find the path to the hearts of the students. Try to extract their fields of interest, and use this to get to their hearts. This does not mean becoming their friend or flattering them. But we must, all the while, send the message that effort on their parts will lead to results. Many times, their blocks are emotional and not cognitive. They are the expression of failed education starting in kindergarten, followed by the failure of the teaching staffs, administration, parents, and neighbors, who told them their whole lives that "you're a failure, you won't amount to anything." And like a self-fulfilling prophecy, that is how they behave. They act according to the label that was placed on them years before they can even remember.

I would suggest completely abolishing all special classrooms. The children need to learn how to handle the real world. Not an imaginary one. If a student is having trouble in a regular classroom, we will get them all the help they need: through tutoring, extra lessons, etc.. Special classrooms for "weak students" will perpetuate their label for themselves, and will set a low standard of expectations for themselves. In any case, out in the real world later on, they will have to adjust to the normal standards and might receive assistance from professional figures as necessary. Out there, nobody will cut them any slack.

One of the graduates of the class I previously wrote about, who was considered by the school as lacking basic learning skills, got lucky and went off to play soccer abroad. He received an offer from a university in the US to play and learn on their campus. This "unsuccessful" student, who did not speak a word of English and was considered hopeless, learned the language in two months and passed the entry exams. He turned out to be a brilliant, unusually motivated student. And if you wanted proof for what I'm saying, there you go.

And now let us move on to you, each and every one of you. You too behave exactly according to the messages you received about yourselves. They said you lacked self-confidence, that you are gentle, considerate, that you must be "good kids" who must behave according to certain rules of conduct. These labels, all of which were said with good intentions and honesty, are limits that were set for you some time in your childhood, they are chains that bind you. They bind your creativity, your bravery, your initiative. Break free of them. Be anything you choose to be. Remember, there is no limit to your abilities, and there is no code regarding how, what or when to do something.

Nobody is checking up on you, and nobody can be your policeman, in any field. The world is all open to you for the taking. Any road you take (even if it seems crazy, lacking any chance or logic and so on), the universe will support you because it is your choice.

From a certain age in life, almost everything is the result of our choices. Anyone who says, "I have no choice," and, "I can't change it," that, "reality is limiting me," or, "I have responsibilities that prevent me from changing"—is mostly relying on excuses. It's true, there are extreme situations in life that are forced on us and almost completely prevent our ability to choose, like a disease, a plague, a global economic crisis and so on. But these are unusual circumstances. In most cases, fear is what holds us back, the limits we place on our own consciousness.

*** 

It is possible we do not want change badly enough; it is possible we are afraid of dealing with the difficulties along the way. It is possible we receive "benefits" from our weaknesses, from the unwanted reality we are tied to. In the end, it is up to us to try and leave a place where we are not satisfied and go somewhere else.

# CHAPTER 30

# There Are Countless Fish in the Human Sea

**As a sworn sea lover, I never stop marveling at the tremendous variety of fish in the sea. No fish looks like another, even if they are very similar. Even those that look identical, are totally different from one another. And they all live in harmony. If so, let us picture human society as one enormous sea.**

I would like to ask that we look around and see this "human sea." Human society is made up of countless people, each one special and one-of-a-kind. Each one of us has a different genetic makeup and set of unique abilities. Each one of us grew up and was educated in a different home and experienced a childhood unique to them. Each one of us has different characteristics, pleasures, preferences, ways of thinking and physical appearances. Just as there is no fish similar to another and no flower identical to another.

We are all God's flowers, the height of creation, the most intelligent creatures of the universe. Remember this when judging others (or yourselves). Remember that you are examining them through your eyes, through your emotional system, based on the memories impressed upon you, your emotional needs and scars, the traditions you were raised on, your religious beliefs and the cultural codes you grew up with. You must understand this basic and fundamental law: other people act and think from their unique perspectives, based on their specific memories, the culture they live in and their human uniqueness.

*Rabbi Menachem Mendel of Kotzk, founder of the Kotzk Hassidic sect in Judaism during the 19th century, said: "Just as you can tolerate the fact that your fellow's face is not similar to yours, so, too, should you be able to tolerate that your fellow's opinions are not similar to yours."*

Why do we get frustrated when other people do not see things the same way that we do? Other people can absolutely not be similar to us. They must be different in their DNA, in the hard disk of their soul. All of human beauty and human creation is compiled of a mosaic of diversity. Herein lies the power of human society. Diversity is not a disadvantage. On the contrary, it is a means for social progress and the complex problem-solving that characterizes our world.

As written in the Babylonian Talmud, Section Damages, tract Sanhedrin (page 38, 71): "One person is different from another in three ways: In voice, in appearance, and in thought."

It is important that we respect people who are different from us, that we are accepting, and that we make society one that is accepting and humanly diverse. In this way, society will become more tolerant, but also richer in cultural shades and more successful. It is the very differences between us that create the complex products of human culture, science, academic research and art. Today it is known that in order to solve complex problems of any kind, there is need for different and various methods, and different approaches and ways of thinking.

In this context, German philosopher and poet Friedrich Nietzsche said: "The surest way to corrupt a youth is to instruct him to hold in higher esteem those who think alike than those who think differently."

***

Remember and memorize: diversity is an advantage, not a disadvantage. It is not a barrier but a helpful tool for human society.

# CHAPTER 31

## The Messengers in Our Lives

**Every person encounters people who are meant to play a significant role in their lives. Oftentimes, the person is unaware of the significance of knowing or meeting them, and only after some time, in hindsight, they understand the part they played in their lives.**

Sometimes, the "messenger" stays in our lives for a long time, sometimes they are gone as quickly as they came after fulfilling their role, and sometimes it is the people we have a negative connection with, who have come into our lives to teach us a lesson so we can change the course of our lives.

To clarify my point, I will bring here two examples:

**Example A:** often we long to renew a lost connection with people from our past, but emotional blocks stop us from doing so. Sometimes, this is baggage from the past: fear, worry, lack of confidence about the other person's desire for a connection with us and so on. I must emphasize that the reasons will always be emotional, never technical. Take, for example, a woman who hasn't seen her childhood friends in twenty years and never struck up the courage to reach out to them. That same woman is invited to a birthday party thrown by the partner of one of her childhood friends. This partner is the messenger, the efficient agent who led to this joint meeting of the group of friends. At this party, our heroine meets her childhood friends that she missed so dearly, and the connection between them is renewed. We see that her friend's partner served as the righteous messenger. His role was to bring her together with her childhood friends.

Example B: sometimes, meeting a close friend from our past can make us reflect on the reality of our lives and what we wish to change. This loaded meeting can bring to the surface old stresses, fears, anxieties, dreams, hopes and old accounts, and mostly will make the person face themselves in the mirror and force them to look inwards. A meeting like this may be crucial and dramatic for both sides, and will usually change both their lives.

Our lives, supposedly, are made up of routine, but this routine is rich with events, experiences and symbols, which we are usually unaware of, and they get swallowed in the gloom of our lives. It is important that we are attentive to the universe and the messages it sends us in all kinds of ways. These ways can vary: a random newspaper article, a movie, a billboard, a random meeting with a stranger during which we will receive a message for our lives, a radio show and so on.

We often play the role of messenger in the lives of others. Many years ago, when I was a young mother and I felt frustrated about giving up my career and self-fulfillment, I spoke with a distant friend who was in a similar situation. She felt ongoing frustration due to the fact that her motherhood was blocking her path for developing a fulfilling career. A year after our meeting, my friend opened a workshop for Judaica and stained glass artworks. Her business flourished for twenty years, and every time we met, she thanked me for that random conversation we had. She claims that talking to me pushed her to open the business, whose products were sold abroad, and without the encouragement from me she never would have dared go in that professional direction. And so, turns out that for that woman I played the role of messenger who led to a turning point in her life and career.

The obvious conclusion: we must be alert to the words and actions of others and listen to them carefully. Often, they hold the keys to our happiness. They shine a light on an area we haven't thought about and were not aware of, and we mustn't discount their words. Coincidental meetings and "insignificant" statements can apparently change our lives, and they are not coincidental at all. They were sent to us by fate/ the universe in order to guide us on the path of life and so we should use them. Let us open our hearts and emotions to our surroundings and receive the hidden messages that the universe sends us.

***

Let us finish with a few words from Noam Horev's book "A Draft of Happiness:"

"In all of our lives, there are temporary people circulating. People who will not go with us hand in hand until the end. People who came into our lives for a limited time for a specific purpose. The temporary people arrive exactly in the moment that we need them. They come to give us a lesson. To teach us something about ourselves." (Noam Horev, "A Draft of Happiness," self-published, 2019, translated from the original Hebrew)

# CHAPTER 32

# Beware, Energy Vampires!

**There are people who have, justifiably so, earned the title "energy vampires." This refers to people with inflated egos, who are frustrated, tired and weary, and who have the ability to drain others of their energy. They will always be in the stance of opposition, will express criticism and have an inner outlook of cynicism and contempt.**

Normally, these types of people sit on the fence and do not take any active or positive part in the game of life. They are full of complaints and present themselves as those who know better than everyone what will work and what won't (usually what won't). They will always thwart any initiative and will create the atmosphere of pessimism and lack of action. Due to the fact that they are aware of their bleak emotional situation, which prevents them from acting, creating and advancing, they will always try to influence those around them to behave and think like them. Otherwise, they will feel inferior (justifiably) to optimism, and to the joy of creating and advancing in others. These people will always voice their opinions, and always in opposition: against the plan, against the schedule, against rational, against everything. Never for something. Their negative attitude castrates and prevents movement toward any kind of change.

For all these reasons, it is important to recognize this quality in their personality and stay away from them and their influence.

### What should we do if we encounter these people in the framework of our professional commitments?

It is recommended to keep contact with them to the bare minimum. If your professional connection does not allow this, it is best not to respond to their incessant criticism and try your best to ignore and "not hear" their critical noise. It is important not to get caught up in an argument with them, which will not help make progress but rather bring it to a halt. In general, we must stand strongly and steadily in our place and not get swept away into an argument with them. We can allow them to speak and let off steam, and then carry out what we intended to do.

A wise manager in an organization will know how to identify these people, those who hold him or her back from setting processes in motion, and neutralize them. A wise individual will know how to recognize these people in their personal life and neutralize their influence.

### And what should we do if they are part of our environment?

Almost all of us have people in our environment that are able to weaken us. Our interpersonal connection with them often makes us feel distress, anger, frustration, feelings of inferiority and other negative emotions. In many cases they do not operate with the intent of hurting us, and they are not aware of their negative power that works against us. In spite of this, our relationship with them is volatile, charged with negative emotions and energies that take us backward instead of forward.

What all the negative emotions, which we experience as a result of this relationship, have in common is— is the fact that they burden us, harm our life energy and joy of life, our vitality, self-image, self-esteem, and motivation to act. These people "guzzle up" our positive energy and block us from development and growth.

On a side note, it is said that there are some people whose personalities are so strong and stable (and some will say even obtuse), that there is no person in the world that can hurt them and nothing can crack their sense of emotional calm and deeply rooted self-confidence. Aren't they lucky... I tend to believe that most humans are vulnerable, in one way or another, even if they do not let emotions rule their lives.

The people with whom we have what we consider to be a negative relationship, may turn out to have good qualities in the company of other people and show care, compassion and tolerance to others. This means that these people are not necessarily negative, but rather our relationship with them brings out the more destructive aspects of their personalities. We will never know why, and probably neither will they. It is rooted deep at the root of the iceberg of their complex psychological psyches.

Mystics will say that these people came into our world to teach us a lesson, and for that they are doing us a great service. I tend to accept this outlook, which claims that there are no coincidences in our world and they are filling an important role in our lives. And yet, it is important that we know how to protect ourselves from their negative influence, which might block our progress and growth: the moment we identify the negative results of the relationship, we must lessen our physical and emotional interaction with them as much as possible, in order to protect ourselves and safeguard our psyches.

*In this context, Maimonides wrote in "Mishneh Torah," his commentary on Jewish philosophy and law: "A person should associate with the righteous and be constantly in the company of the wise, so as to learn from their deeds. Conversely, he should keep away from the wicked who walk in darkness, so as not to learn from their deeds."*

On the other side of things, we must look for and create relationships that are good for us with people who appreciate our personalities and send us positive and empowering messages about ourselves. People who accept us as we are, without criticism and judgment, regarding our human complexities. People we can trust to stand by us through good times and bad. People who are supportive of our successes, who are happy when we are happy and successful, and who we are happy for when they are successful, or in the words of Winnie the Pooh in Alan Alexander Milne's book: "A day without a friend is like a pot without a single drop of honey left inside."

Look for the people who will empower you and plant in you the confidence in your ability to achieve your goals, in people who will strengthen your sense of capability. Close your ears to words that harm your belief in yourself.

I will tell you a personal story. Around thirty years ago, I started learning for my master's degree. I was after the birth of my youngest daughter and had two other small children at home, a six-year-old daughter and a ten-year-old son. Handling raising the children, work and housework was complicated, and I believe any woman can relate to me on this issue. During a seminar, as part of my studies, I became friendly with an older woman who had a senior position at one of the municipalities, who heard my personal story and did not really encourage me, to say the least. She repeatedly said to me "You won't be able to manage," "It's crazy with three kids at home," "There's no way," and similar disheartening words.

After few months I quit school. Indeed I felt I wasn't able to withstand the load. Obviously her words were not the main reason I gave up, but in the complex situation I was functioning in, her words had a destructive effect. I completed my master's degree after several years, and continued straight on to my doctorate.

I share this story to demonstrate that for a person who is already feeling distress, it is enough for someone to mutter a few discouraging words, and they will collapse.

On the other hand, a person who strengthens and encourages their friend who is in a difficult and complicated situation—might help them soar. And so, choose relationships that will benefit you. Life brings us challenging and complex situations, and it is important that we have people by our side who will support us, root for us, people who will help us succeed through demanding times in our lives and empower us.

As the French author and moralist François de La Rochefoucauld wrote: "One must listen if one wishes to be listened to."

I would like to address the dimension of gender. Women have a harder time advancing in life (due to several reasons that are not appropriate to elaborate on here). This is why, I believe that women, especially successful women, have a responsibility to other women: helping them get ahead, encouraging them, making them believe in their abilities and being a role model for them. Female solidarity and sisterhood are the cornerstones of the feminist movement. Strengthen your female sisters at every opportunity you get.

\*\*\*

And for the rest of my dear friends, I will repeat: your quality of life depends largely on the personal relationships you nurture during your lives. Choose to have by your sides positive and empowering people, those who will strengthen you when you are faced with the challenges of life.

# CHAPTER 33

# Trust and a Healthy Work Environment

**Trust between human-beings is one of the most important things in life. It is like an unwritten contract between partners, colleagues, a manager and his or her employees, a commander and his or her soldiers, a doctor and his or her patients, a business owner and his or her clients, a country and its citizens and a state and its institutions and so on.**

*The Scottish author George MacDonald said: "To be trusted is a greater compliment than to be loved."*

The basis of this trust is the mutual assumption that both sides see transparency and honesty as the single standard for thinking and acting. Both sides think in terms of transparency, honesty, decency and good will. They both agree on the principles of justice and humaneness. They both believe that each one of them stands behind their honesty and brings out the best in themselves.

The moment the basis of this trust is undermined (usually when one side breaks the unwritten agreement and behaves dishonestly) both sides will have a hard time returning to a mutual system of co-operation. When one side does not believe in the honesty and good intentions of the other side, they will not see them as a real partner, professionally or personally. The moment one side loses the basic trust necessary for joint creation, they will stop being a potential partner.

*The German philosopher Friedrich Nietzsche wrote about this: "I'm not upset that you lied to me, I'm upset that from now on I can't believe you."*

*And an Irish saying says: "When mistrust comes in, love goes out."*

Personal leadership and national leadership must embody the values of honesty and equity. A leadership that is based on intrigue, manipulations, lies, schemes and the method of divide and conquer, is a leadership with no legitimacy to exist, does not have a strong standing and is not rooted firmly in reality. It is based on false appearances of cooperation and action. The same goes for professional conduct. This type of conduct, which is based on hypocrisy and lies, cannot last very long, since it is not based on purposeful and thorough work.

*Perhaps that is what Niccolò Machiavelli, the Italian statesman and philosopher, meant when he said: "Whoever steals a handkerchief goes to jail, whoever steals a country, becomes a Duke."*

An organization, state, or institution that take on negative phenomena that manifest as everyone mistrusting everyone, informing on each other, belligerence and manipulations, is a corrupt system, which in the end harms the organization itself, and will be the one to cause it to fail. Beyond the fact that these phenomena are immoral, they are like a cancer in the body of the organization. A manager who uses these corrupt methods to control his or her people, will end up losing their leadership and the institution they are running. It is typical of this degeneration to pervade inward, to all roles and branches of the organization.

*The French philosopher Charles Louis Montesquieu wrote about this: "The corruption of each government begins almost always with the corruption of its principle."*

*The Greek philosopher Aristotle said: "The basis of a democratic state is liberty."*

*And Israeli philosopher Asa Kasher stated: "In a democratic state, the leadership is first and foremost a leadership of decency."*

\*\*\*

It is fundamentally simple: a clean work environment is a transparent work environment, based on honesty and fairness, excellent professional performance, and backing up and giving credit to the people who are doing their jobs.

# CHAPTER 34

# We All Need Encouragement

**We all need encouragement, a kind word and praise for our efforts and accomplishments. Encouragement meaning recognition and appreciation from our environment for our qualities and performance. This encouragement gives us self-esteem and the strength to keep going on the path we are on.**

*A wise Japanese saying says: "One kind word can warm three winter months."*

It's easy to say, "Be where you feel encouraged." This may seem like a trivial statement, but everyone should examine how often they find themselves, coincidentally or not, in a place that robs them of their energy. Places in which they do not get the encouragement and appreciation they deserve.

- **Encouragement in a romantic relationship:** many people stay in relationships that are not supportive of them and sometimes even harmful. They will feel miserable all their lives, and this will affect their health (this is not the place to explain the complicated reasons why people stay in relationships that are not rewarding for them emotionally and are sometimes harmful. Most of the time it stems from fear: fear of sustaining oneself financially, lack of confidence in being able to survive on one's own, and fear of hurting the children).

It is important that everyone know—and be convinced—that they deserve love and appreciation in their relationship. There is no reason in the world that justifies any other treatment from one's partner, and it is a shame to stay in a negative, energy-draining relationship instead of a positive one that is nurtured with love and positive energy.

- **Encouragement in the workplace:** it is best for us, of course, to work in an organization that deems our professional performances good and successful, and so, motivation will increase naturally. Working at a place that does not give praise to our professional efforts and accomplishments makes us feel frustrated, distressed, and taken advantage of. Over time, these feelings can harm our emotional and physical strength.

A smart manager will invest in nurturing their employees, highlight their achievements and (metaphorically) pat them on the back. They will strengthen their self confidence and praise them for their professional achievements and their contribution to the organization. That's how they will secure their continued investment.

Every manager should remember: an investment that's based on the true and honest will and intent of the employee, will always be better than an investment based on duty, fear or monetary incentives.

- **A life full of encouragement:** it is important to be around people who are supportive of our abilities and send us positive messages about our abilities in any area: career, academic studies, business, love, raising children. We should choose those who tell us "You have the skills and abilities to succeed." These words will create reality.

And in continuation to what has been said, we should also remove people from our lives. We should remove those who make us feel lack of confidence in ourselves and doubt our abilities. We are talking about our physical and mental health, and so it is our duty to ourselves.

There are people who have been born into families where they felt emotionally deprived. Families where the parents were not impressed by their children, did not strengthen their sense of self and did not give them the love and warmth they needed to grow up to be emotionally healthy and happy adults. A child like this, once grown up, will feel their whole lives as if they are lacking their "security shield" or "security blanket" which is so vital for life. Life is full of struggles, successes and failures. A person who did not gain emotional confidence in their childhood, must seek treatment, invest in their spirituality, and surround themselves with loving and encouraging people who will send them positive energy. They would be better off in places where they will receive support, love, warmth and encouragement.

Nevertheless, we must remember that from the moment we become adults, it is our responsibility to take care of ourselves and strengthen our psyche. This will allow us to lean on our own emotional support and not on external reinforcement. We cannot fix the past, but the present is completely in our hands, and is what is important and relevant to our lives today.

\*\*\*

*Let us summarize this with the words of the Greek philosopher Epicte-tus, who said: "The key is to keep company only with people who uplift you, whose presence calls forth your best."*

# CHAPTER 35

## Internal and External

**It has been written in the Book of Proverbs "Grace is deceitful and beauty is vain." This isn't to say that external beauty is unimportant. The opposite, beauty and an aesthetic appearance are highly meaningful components for making a first impression, and beauty in general can give a person comfort. As it is written in our sources, "Three matters give a person comfort, and they are: A beautiful abode, a beautiful wife, and beautiful vessels." However...**

Act wisely in your lives and do not blindly follow first appearances. Over-cordiality in a first meeting with a stranger should set off your defense mechanism. Someone who is confident does not feel the need to impress others every time they meet, or the need to receive external approval for their personality and abilities.

This doesn't mean we should be bad-tempered toward people in our first meeting. A smile and warm expression are always important and make a positive first impression, but on the other hand, the people you meet for the first time will not become your best friends right away, and you won't be sharing personal or discrete information with them.

Always try and seek out a person's soul beneath their external appearance. A person's beautiful soul is what matters, not their looks. I have encountered people whose arrogance and sometimes maliciousness, lead them throughout their lives, but their appearances are pleasant and they deceive those around them. Do not blindly follow words of flattery. Be hesitant. You are allowed to examine the person in your own way before trusting them.

*Stendhal, of the great French writers, wrote: "But what is beauty? The ability to give you pleasure."*

A friendship may rise or fall based on such trust. A friendship that is not based on full trust is not friendship, but a superficial relationship built on personal interests, one which lacks mutual empathy and commitment. Learn to distinguish between the superficial relationships you maintain in your life, which serve you in different areas, and a brave friendship, a soulmate connection that withstands the test of time and survives crises.

Life will teach you to choose your friends. Choose them based on these facts:

Can you fully trust them? Are they mentally healthy, spiritually stable individuals who will strengthen you, listen to you and give you support and encouragement in your time of need?

\*\*\*

In general, surround yourselves with healthy people, physically and emotionally. People with "joie de vivre," who are happy with their lot and who don't carry even an ounce of jealousy toward others. These people will give your life good energy and you will give to them as well.

# CHAPTER 36

# A Balanced or a Destructive Friendship

**Albert Camus, the French writer and philosopher, said so beautifully about friendship:** *"Don't walk in front of me, I may not follow. Don't walk behind me, I may not lead. Walk beside me, be my friend."*

Our relationships, whether romantic or platonic, should be equal, symmetrical, mutual; there cannot be a relationship where only one side gives while the other side takes. It cannot be that one side should share their personal life, while the other remains closed off, remote and emotionally blocked. It cannot be that one side is honest and open, while the other closed and introverted. It is unacceptable for there to be an emotional and intimate discourse from one side while the other responds in a technical manner. It cannot be that one side gives of themselves physically and emotionally while the other side spares their physical strengths and emotional resources. It cannot be that one side is committed and the other is not.

*The Roman philosopher and statesman Cicero, spoke of the importance of friendship: "Robbing life of friendship is like robbing the world of the sun." And the Greek philosopher Aristotle described it in the words: "Friendship is a single soul dwelling in two bodies."*

Due to the complexity of the term "friendship," I suggest we all clarify it for ourselves: What does this term mean to us? For one person it means spending time together over a nice breakfast, a trip, clothes shopping or a trip abroad, while all done with humor and joy. For another person, friendship mostly means sharing, acceptance and encouragement, showing interest and giving emotional support at any given time. And indeed, you do not always see eye to eye with your friends. Too many people experience the anguish of an asymmetrical friendship. When they give to their friends encouragement and support and sometimes even physical help during a crisis, but do not get similar treatment in return when they need it. Their "good" friends disappear into thin air when they need them emotionally.

*Homer, of the great Greek poets, wrote in "The Odyssey": "For a friend with a sympathetic heart, is worth no less than a brother."*

*The musician Jim Morrison, singer of "The Doors," said: "A friend is someone who gives you total freedom to be yourself."*

**Between friends:** It is important to understand the nature of a person before initiating a friendship with them. And we better decide who our friends are based on their personality and not their social status, bank account, the prestige they are privileged to, etc.. All these things are irrelevant to us and our relationship with them. Even social attributes of theirs that stand out, like being outgoing, having a good sense of humor or being the life of the party—all these are irrelevant when a person is in distress and needs a listening ear or a shoulder to lean on.

*Here is what American politician and writer Benjamin Franklin wrote about this: "Be slow in choosing a friend, slower in changing."*

Every relationship must be symmetrical. Each side must feel as though they are giving their all to the friendship. The moment one side feels emptiness or lack, and lives with the sense that they are not receiving in the same way that they are giving, something is wrong in the relationship. This is an asymmetrical relationship, and I am referring to an internal feeling of one of the sides (obviously, this term is not objective. Some people give of themselves to their maximum abilities, and we must believe them that these are the limits of their abilities).

**In a romantic relationship:** a relationship between a couple must first and foremost be based on a friendship between the couple. But what happens when one of the partners feels that there is no symmetry in the relationship?

In this situation a few possibilities may develop:

1. The side that feels a lack will seek out other sources to fill their emotional batteries. They may develop a close and intimate friendship with a member of their sex or the opposite sex (a friendship that doesn't have to be necessarily romantic) as a replacement for the emotional intimacy they feel they are lacking.
2. They may remain in their sense of lack, which will become chronic, and fill it with a thousand-and-one activities, such as learning, friends, work, food, TV, classes and so on. Anything to escape the feelings of distress and emptiness.
3. They may choose to leave their partner.

It is important to remember that none of us can change another person. A relationship, whether platonic or romantic, is built on the will of both parties. Partners that feel emptiness and stay in the relationship, do so out of choice. It is important that they know that they have other options to choose from.

And there is another type of friendship: a destructive friendship. This is a relationship in which one side not only isn't growing thanks to it, but is losing strength, power, confidence, and internal energy due to the friendship.

When we identify a person, who for whatever reason destabilizes our power, weakens us, makes us feel burdened, with low self-esteem or anguish and other negative feelings toward ourselves—we must examine what exactly in the relationship with them is causing this. If we identify that this is happening because they are feeling superior to us, arrogant, judgmental, canceling our achievements and are lacking support for us—then we must come to the right conclusions and stay away. This is our obligation to ourselves.

\*\*\*

In a sentence: Stay away from relationships that are not mutual and do not enrich you, and from people who make you feel bad.

# CHAPTER 37

# Stand Up for Your Dignity

**We must always stand up for our dignity. It is our most valuable asset, and we must not let anyone trample it. Not a person in the world has the right to hurt us or our right to express our opinions freely, not even in the name of public or national interest, family honor, social appearances, respecting one's parents and so forth.**

This does not mean that you are immune to criticism. Constructive criticism is legitimate and even desirable when it pertains to a specific event or to the way you behaved about a certain matter. But learn to make the distinction: criticism is legitimate when it addresses an action or conduct, but not when it pertains to your personality or your value. Do not agree to be canceled as humans, as thinking people, as people who can have a dialogue. Do not agree for people to tell you that you are inferior, that you are not capable, that you lack talent, that you are not good enough for...

*Author Mark Twain said: "Keep away from people who try to belittle your ambitions. The really great make you feel that you, too, can become great."*

Never agree to be disrespected, humiliated or belittled. Do not let anyone in the world do this, even though your self-confidence does not depend on it. Silence in the face of insult and belittling oneself gives legitimacy and power to the arbitrariness, humiliation and maliciousness of the other person.

*The Roman philosopher Seneca, wrote: "What you think about yourself is much more important than what others think about you."*

*This is what Thomas Jefferson, one of the United States' Founding Fathers and the third president, wrote in the US declaration of independence: "We hold these truths to be self-evident, that all men are created equal, that they are endowed by their Creator with certain unalienable Rights, that among these are Life, Liberty and the pursuit of Happiness."*

\*\*\*

Your self-confidence and sense of capability stem from the deep inner knowledge regarding what you are worth, and there is no need for external approval. And yet, this does not mean you should allow others to mock you, humiliate you, insult you, or belittle you. Return it in favor!

# CHAPTER 38

## Set Your Egos Aside

**Our lives are full of challenges, missions and tasks of different levels of importance. The way we handle them, more often than not, stems from the way our ego behaves.**

Many of us are unaware that the way we conduct ourselves in the face of challenges serves our ego, and not the goal. Take for example an organization where a certain strategy of operation has been chosen and it includes all professional staff members. You, as the team leader, suddenly find out that one of the team members did not act according to the plan but took their own initiative. By doing so, he showed selfishness and lack of collegiality, withheld information from his friends and did not act within his authority, while ignoring the administration's instructions. The other team members are enraged (rightfully so), and demand severe judgment for their rogue friend. You are considering their request to have an open discussion on the topic and throw the facts in his face. How will you choose to act?

First of all, you must decide what you want to get out of the rogue colleague.

- First option: You wish to reprimand the person, make them see the error of their ways and have them promise that it will never happen again. Meaning, choosing the option that serves your and your team's wounded egos, as well as your need for retribution, and so you will raise the topic in an open discussion, where the rogue team member will be attacked and humiliated in a lynch-like environment. You and your team's thirst for vengeance will be satisfied, but what's next? It is possible that this move will mark the end of this person's job in the organization, or alternatively will taint the team atmosphere and harm the quality of their joint work. Think of the future: Could you possibly get this team member to continue his work in a cooperative, effective and proper way? Can you preserve the team's cohesiveness and the positive energy within it in order to lead to the creation of a better product?

By means of group retribution, you might lose the rogue member, physically and metaphorically. You will not be able to bring him on board in the future. You and your friends may grant freedom to your feelings of anger and vengeance, however, the real purpose of clearing the air and arranging proper working procedures, will be lost. The feeling of humiliation, exclusion and contempt that your friend will feel, will neutralize any chance of continued work together in the future.

Second option: You can neutralize your ego—your feelings of anger and need for retribution—for the good of continued effective and successful teamwork.

In this case, you would call in that rogue team member for a private conversation, where you would lay out all your accusations and inquire about their motives. In this way, you will achieve your actual goal without embarrassing them publicly and without humiliating them. Or in other words, without pleasing your ego and indulging your urge for retaliation.

*Ralph Waldo Emerson, the American philosopher and writer, said about this: "For every minute you are angry you lose sixty seconds of happiness."*

*The French writer and satirist Francois de La Rrochefoucauld said: "It's easier to be wise for others than for ourselves" (from the book "Maxims"). And he also said: "Mediocre minds usually dismiss anything which reaches beyond their own understanding."*

*Here is another example: A coworker insulted you publicly in front of your other colleagues. You are capable of returning an eye for an* eye and humiliating them in a similar situation. But what have you achieved? You repaid them in kind, with malice, just as they did to you. Raise yourself to a higher humane and moral standard than them and don't get pulled down to their lowly and disgraceful level. Restrain your ego. Rise above the need for retaliation. It is so easy to get dragged down to the shameful behavior of other people. Instead, choose to display honor and wisdom and share with them your opinion about their behavior in a private conversation using stern words. It is probable they will learn a lesson from you about compassion and mutual respect.

The philosopher Jean-Jacques Rousseau wrote in his book "The Reveries of a Solitary Walker": "Innocence is the only support I depend on in my sufferings, how much more wretched then should I make myself, if relinquishing this last, this powerful resource, I substituted wickedness in its place?"

\*\*\*

Our lives are full of such examples. A reaction coming from anger and rage will always serve the ego and the deeper emotions that were hurt, and demand immediate response to the insult. Think for a few moments before responding. Do not be tempted to serve your hurt pride and do not give in to the need for retaliation and the need to always be right. Leave your ego where it belongs, think about what you want to achieve long-term, and then respond in a way that will serve your true goal.

# CHAPTER 39

# Life is Not a Display Window

**Sadly, we live in a world today where social networks have become a display window, where people mostly show their external beauty, assets, various achievements, different pastimes and glamorous lives.**

For example, I recently read in an online magazine about the life of a wealthy woman. The woman described in great detail the reality of her fascinating life, which includes shopping in Israel and abroad, trips and hobbies, which of course, involve spending large sums of money, such as collecting art, designing expensive furniture and so on. Obviously all of this woman's items are first class in the world—bags, shoes, clothes and such. There is not enough space here to cover it all. It disturbed me that nothing was said in the article about this respectable woman's value system. I would have been happy to read about whether she did good things for the community, for people in need; and in general, what is the set of principles by which she lives. In my opinion, the magazine failed here by presenting such a shallow model for life, and role model for their readers.

Indeed, there are those among us who live their lives as if in a display window. All their actions, whether consciously or not, have the intention of receiving approval, support and admiration of others. They are completely disconnected from their true feelings. They, like the woman in the article, need to constantly get approval from society that they are good enough, fashionable enough, talented enough, etc.. They themselves do not believe in their talents, and from that comes their uncontrollable urge to be famous. They lack basic confidence in themselves and their inner happiness depends on outside approval. And so, naturally they live in a constant state of frustration.

In my humble opinion, each one of us carries in our hearts personal and social scars from childhood. I reached this conclusion after an elementary school reunion. I remember this one girl in our grade who was really popular. She was always surrounded by friends thanks to her smarts and beauty. Her name carried a special aura for many years to come. Unexpectedly, I spoke with her at length during the class reunion, and we created this open and friendly dialogue. To my surprise, she told me about her miserable childhood due to severe family problems. She described feelings of loneliness and suffering, to the point where I found it hard to believe that this was the same girl that we all identified as the epitome of perfection and happiness.

From this I reached the conclusion that only the person themselves knows their true state of happiness. Never rely on the reports of others, or a glamorous image. Ask the person themselves. Listen to them and you will receive the real answer.

Look for happiness within you, in your consciousness, inside you. Do not listen to society's instruction. Go simply with what you feel. Society cannot dictate to you how you are supposed to feel. Sometimes, the outer wrapping is pretty but the inside is rotten.

We live in a global world that is ruled by various social networks: Facebook, Instagram, Tik Tok, Twitter and others. These social networks have become display windows for many of us. They answer our need to share with the world our personal lives, trips, leisure activities, family occasions and so on. They are a tool to help us grow our social circles and help many people lessen their feelings of loneliness.

Without a doubt, the social networks have led to the democratization of the masses. The ability to express different opinions about various topics on social networks, influences all areas of our lives. Politics, economy, art and culture, leisure culture, health and every other area of our lives. However, social networks have become a public courthouse, a virtual town square, an arena for defamation, humiliation and shaming. "Fake news" is posted on social networks by self-serving figures who cause dire harm to people, companies, parties, organizations, communities and even countries. It is crucial that we handle the information on social networks with care, and examine it with topical and factual criticism.

Remember: do not mix up your Facebook "friends" with your real-life friends—the ones who will strengthen you in times of crisis, carry your pain and be there physically for you when you need them. Social networks are an important and legitimate tool for marketing and promoting your professional, business, commercial, artistic and academic activities. They are an excellent tool for life in the 21st century, but are certainly not a substitute for dealing with real life.

\*\*\*

Make sure that the internal content of your life is rich and full of good and positive energy. Live your life with the people who love you and support you and love them back; it doesn't matter at all if these people are young, old, with this social standing or that. Your happiness flows from your well of emotions, not from a material source.

# CHAPTER 40

# Seek Out Human Power Plants

**Albert Schweitzer, the 1952 Nobel Peace Prize winning physician and philosopher, said:** *"Example is not the main thing in influencing others. It is the only thing."* **I suggest that each one of us choose for ourselves a "human star" or "human power plant." Meaning, a person who will serve as our role model and inspiration.**

This person will be a mentor and spiritual guide for us, and we will aspire to reach their moral level and professional and spiritual achievements. They will set the "human standard" to which we aspire, and so they must have personal qualities worthy of emulating.

They will serve as our guide for life, we will consult with them in our time of need, receive encouragement from them, and alternatively, hear about other paths for life than the ones we have taken so far. All this, without judgment or criticism from their part, but only the desire to help us. They will be to us what a rabbi or priest is for religious people.

They may be our father, mother, friend, superior at work, a colleague or university professor. They might even be someone subordinate to us professionally, or someone on a lower social or economic level.

There is no significance to their economic, professional or social status.

Religious people are very lucky. To them, everything is written in the holy Torah, and if needed they consult a rabbi. Everything that happens in their lives—the good, the bad—comes from God. In this way, they deal with the events of their lives with greater acceptance than those who do not believe.

Every person must have a solid set of incontrovertible moral values. I liken these values to a kind of "moral blanket" that covers us our whole lives. It gives us warmth and protection, valuable boundaries, confidence, the sense that something good is enveloping us and safe-guarding us, both as individuals and as a society. This value system keeps our lives defined with clear moral boundaries. And just as a blanket sometimes covers and uncovers us, it's possible we might test these boundaries during our lives, we might deviate a little past the limits we set for ourselves, but it's likely that after not too long we will put the blanket back in its place.

The warmth of this "blanket" is like the human warmth we will emit to our surroundings, and that it will emit back to us. Our human warmth will not remain with us alone, but will be directed at our family members, at the people we love, at the community we live in and at the people around us.

In life, we are commanded to help those in need as best we can. If a person turns to us for advice or help, whether physical, financial, professional or social, we must do everything in our power to help them. Any assistance we give them—we will receive tenfold from the universe. A person who cannot give of themselves will not get anything from society or from the universe.

*The author Charles Dickens said: "No one is useless in this world who lightens the burdens of another."*

*And Roman writer and philosopher Cicero stated: "We are not born for ourselves alone."*

\*\*\*

We may be the "human star" for other people. We shall see this as a privileged and sacred duty.

# SECTION 6

## MATTERS OF THE SPIRIT

# CHAPTER 41

# Do Not Give Up On Yourself

**Most of us were raised on the wonderful values of helping others, social solidarity and consideration of others. However, we must admit that in this complex, competitive and modern world, a person must first serve their own needs and fight for themselves.**

As a member of the Scouts, I was ingrained with basic principles of humaneness that are the foundation of the moral worldview that has accompanied me my whole life. In the education system where I learned, and at home, I was taught to always operate while looking around me in order not to harm the rights and feelings of other people. I wouldn't dare throw away these wonderful human values. Moreover, these are values that I try to uphold in all circles of my life. That said, during the many years I've lived, I discover, sadly, over and over, that I often tend to give up on myself and put others' needs before my own physical and emotional needs. That is how these values become a double edged sword.

In this complex, competitive and modern world, a person must first serve their own needs and fight for themselves, for their own well-being and to promote their own interests. This is not shameful or arrogant. This is a person's duty to firstly love themselves and promote themselves in any legitimate and non-aggressive way; in a way that will present their advantages (also in relation to the competition), and by way of marketable strategies. They cannot, by any means, rely on others to take care of them in any way—financially, emotionally, socially and even politically. That said, they must place limits on themselves so as not to trample others while they are getting ahead.

Every individual, both man and woman, must cultivate their personal interests, circle of good friends, activities and leisure time with their partners and without. Leisure that will answer their emotional and intellectual needs. It isn't fair to cast on those close to us the task of keeping us happy and interested at all times, in a way that will fill our emotional and cognitive void.

A person's backbone must be the person themselves. It is not right to have one's partner or other external person be the staff they lean on. They must stand in their own right, emotionally, mentally, and as much as possible—financially.

*Confucius, the great Chinese philosopher, summed it up in this sentence: "What the superior man seeks, is in himself. What the small man seeks, is in others."*

Wonderful children and sweet grandchildren are the "added bonus" of life. However, I often meet people who define themselves through their children. In my opinion, it is a mistake that they haven't built a rich personality for themselves. As parents and grandparents, they often cancel out themselves and their own needs, and use their economic, physical and emotional resources for the good of their children/ grandchildren.

***

Here I must qualify my words and say, that if it is appropriate for their physical, emotional and intellectual needs—then great. That said, I suggest that these people examine themselves carefully: is their absolute devotion to their children's needs done out of choice, or does it serve as an escape from having to deal with life? Check yourselves on this, too.

# CHAPTER 42

# What Are They Running From?

**Many people live their lives while they are cut off and disconnected from their feelings: they are too busy with their everyday tasks, too afraid, fearful of the demons and spirits hiding deep down in the depths of their souls, and they escape into their busy, intensive lives in order to avoid encountering the scars and pain that are etched in their psyches. Some of them suffer for years from a poor quality of life, anxiety, fears, hindrances and emotional blocks.**

In order to improve their quality of life and overcome the pain and trauma of their past, it is important that they seek professional treatment. This treatment is hard emotionally, since it digs deep into the depths of one's soul, the subconscious, the scars of life, and childhood trauma. That is where the person might encounter the "demons" that are blocking their way in life, the unpleasant experiences they've been trying to forget and suppress for years. However, these difficult experiences that have been etched into our memories and burned into our psyches, will not disappear if we do not treat them. Traumas, particularly from childhood, will accompany us our whole lives, without regard to the dimension of time or space. They are fixed, burned into our psyches and surface in certain situations that echo long-forgotten events.

As a therapist delves into these experiences with the patient, they bring them up from the subconscious to the surface, attribute the correct weight to them, clean and treat the wounds, and put things into the right perspective. Our emotional blocks might open and our quality of life may change beyond recognition. The child within us will return to their natural and appropriate proportions, to the little chest inside us, and there, from our mature viewpoint and life experience, we will give them love and attention.

There are people who are in a constant state of rush throughout their lives, yet they complain about their stressful routines. On the other hand, free time is threatening to them, since it leaves them time to face their emotions. In their spare time, they will seek out different activities, and once again find themselves on the racetrack, and this race may lead them to crash health-wise, emotionally, physically and in their family lives.

A person like this better ask themselves what they are running from. The answer will force them to confront themselves and determine a new daily routine in life, a new set of priorities and true change.

Life sometimes forces us to make changes, even if we did not willingly initiate them. Sometimes it is a disease, either of our own or of a beloved relative. Sometimes, these are unwanted changes that have been forced on us at work or in our relationship, or God forbid, following the loss of a loved one. A change like this will be powerful and meaningful. It will result from a forceful blow on the floor of reality and the ground of life.

\*\*\*

If we survive this forceful blow, then the change we will make will be painful and deep and will shock the doorposts of our lives, but this is also where the chance to live a better life will present itself to us.

# CHAPTER 43

# Feeding the Soul

**Every person is made of body and spirit. The body must be treated with proper nutrition, exercise, rest, meditation, routine checkups and so on. Our souls must be fed with spiritual substance. With culture, with music, and with anything that enriches us and grants our lives meaning.**

The soul is hungry and thirsty for spiritual sustenance. It must find its purpose in life: goals, targets, pleasures, emotional satisfaction—otherwise, the person will be like a wild animal. If a person lives only on a physical level, then they are only half-complete individuals. Their soul is hurting and suffering. It is in a constant state of spiritual lack, and so it cries out at night. It (the subconscious) wakes them.

During the day, a person is busy and troubled by the struggle for survival, making money, family life, and daily troubles. They are not available and do not want to dedicate time and energy to treat their emotional self, their spirit. They are afraid of what they may discover about themselves and their lives if they go in and dig around in the closet of their emotions and childhood. And so, they prefer to avoid searching for the meaning of their lives and the hidden motives that drive them. But their soul will not leave them alone. It demands what it deserves, demands attention, it cries out. That is why there are some people who cannot silence their souls at night. It breaks through the defense shield and thick concrete that they built around their feelings. It hurts them with great force and wakes them up with terrifying dreams, troubling thoughts and constant unrest.

A person cut off from their feelings will avoid having real and honest relationships with those around them, and will have a hard time having an emotionally intimate connection with their partner. They will operate on a physical level, but will never reach an emotional depth in any area of their lives.

*The American dancer and choreographer Katherine Mary Dunham, called for us to find that inner fire within us: "Go within every day and find the inner strength so that the world will not blow your candle out."*

It isn't possible to function and communicate with people, and primarily with yourself, only on the level of need and rational. In the complete person there is unity of body and spirit, and this connection cannot be severed. A person who denies their desires and feelings, is a person who operates without spiritual support, and lacks a true connection to life. They are weak, open to health problems, fatigue and weakness.

Our spiritual backbone is our soul. When it is honest, stable, nourished on a steady and solid basis—so too will our lives. They will be loaded with moral strength, vitality, full of content and meaning.

\*\*\*

Connect with your soul. Start in this very moment the process of connecting it.. Nourish and cultivate it, and it will look after you.

# CHAPTER 44

## An Emotional Energy Reserve

**I am asking you to see your soul as a precious reserve of valuable emotional energy. This human energy, which draws from different sources, is not inexhaustible. That is why it is every person's duty to refill this spiritual reserve, give from it to worthy beloved people, or direct it to doing good deeds for yourselves and for others.**

A person is obligated to involve their soul in all the different activities they do in their life. Deeds that are done without the involvement of the soul are technical, superficial, and, worse, they lack energetic power.

There is this claim that says that professionalism is supposedly lacking emotion, that it is rational, and must not be influenced by emotional motives. I completely disagree. Part of having a soul, as humans do, means acting out of emotion and logic together. A person must feel the cooperation between all their emotions and values in their actions. This is why I disagree with the approach that people who are only rational will function better and reach higher professional achievements. Case in point: a person who lacks professional experience but has great enthusiasm, a vision, passion and ambition, has infinitely higher chances of succeeding than a person with extensive professional knowledge, but who lacks inner strength, enthusiasm, and a deep emotional commitment to the task.

As Marshal Foch, the decorated French commander who served during the First World War, said: "The most powerful weapon on earth is the human soul on fire."

Before you invest emotional energy in an organization, a task or a project, think about what you have to gain from it. I do not necessarily mean physical gain, like a promotion, appreciation, money, etc.. I mean an emotional gain.

It's true, physical needs (such as food, shelter, stability in life, cleanliness and order or money) are indeed very important, but those who think that that's what life is all about are mistaken. A life based on the fulfillment of physical needs alone, is meager, empty, and frustrating—a life without meaning and without a connection to the spirit and to emotional needs. A person who hides, represses, closes off their spirit from connecting to their deeper desires, are likened to a half-person. A person who is not attentive to themselves and their soul, is doomed to quickly wither away.

The soul is like the gas that fuels a car. Without the gas, the car will not move. A person who does not feed their soul, will eventually come to a stop.

You safeguard your money in the bank, but you do not look after your soul and spiritual consciousness. Allow yourselves to occasionally let loose and be silly. Return to being those children you once were, those happy and curious children. Connect with your inner child who knows best about what is right for you and what your purpose is in the world.

Look for the meaning in your life, and it will fill your life with spiritual richness, as the philosopher Shimon Azulay writes: "That moment I switched my aspiration for happiness with the aspiration for meaning was the most defining moment of my life. Meaning is that unique mark that we leave on the world, and so I am busy creating footprints." (from an interview with the newspaper "Globes," 13.10.2016, interviewer: Vered Ramon Rivlin).

***

Give joy to your soul and enrich your spirituality. Take care of it, nurture it and listen to it. Allow yourself to break down and cry every once in a while. Watch a funny movie and crack up with laughter. Do things you love that will fill your heart. Make sure that the glass of your soul is always full.

# CHAPTER 45

# "Worry in a Man's Heart, Let Him Subdue it"

**Each one of us—whether rich or poor, whether famous or ordinary—has several frustrations and burdens in our lives. Moreover, it is usually the people on the higher end of the ladder whose lives are full of frustration, anger and tension as a result of the scope of their political, social or financial activities.**

*Buddha said: "You will not be punished for your anger; you will be punished by your anger."*

What is the intelligent way of dealing with that frustration and tension? How can we overcome objective difficulties and grow ourselves in the face of the complex challenges of our lives?

First of all, we must examine the elements that frustrate us. Apparently this is not a simple task at all. Many people will have a hard time putting their finger on the element causing their frustration and lack of personal fulfillment or their sense of misery. It is possible they will need external therapeutic help in identifying the problem. Other people tend to burst out at those around them (often at those closest to them), and make them their punching bags, which is a great injustice. There are those who, when faced with life's challenges, wrap themselves in a shroud of silence and absorb into their souls the poison of depression, frustration and anger, and will eventually pay for this with their health.

The right way is to let out the negative emotions and troubling burdens. To talk about them with someone close or a professional. Our sages have said "Worry in a man's heart. Let him subdue it." Sometimes, the action of talking and having a dialogue will help relieve the person of a big part of their emotional burden. Sometimes, the person they share their pain with, will also give them emotional support. In other cases, it is best to turn to a professional for help.

Maimonides, who was also a physician, insisted on the importance of receiving emotional assistance in order to overcome the woes of the soul: "What is the remedy for the morally ill? They should go to the wise, for they are the healers of souls. They will heal them by teaching themselves how to acquire proper traits, until they return them to the good path."

In any case, neglecting one's emotional distress due to an "everything will be Okay" mentality, will not only not achieve this goal, but may lead to a crisis as a result of untreated and unresolved frustrations and depression.

*** 

Remember that in moments of frustration, you can turn to friends who will strengthen you and encourage you. Memorize this Swedish proverb: "The best place to find a helping hand is at the end of your own arm."

# CHAPTER 46

# Find Your Emotional Shelter

**It is important that we each have an "emotional shelter." A shelter is a safe space, a place where we can hide from our surroundings without a watchful eye and in total freedom. It is a place—physical or metaphorical—that is good to return to and escape to when things get tough outside.**

What exactly is this emotional shelter? For one person, an emotional shelter may be a hobby that they escape to whenever they can. For another person it may be learning, for a third—solitary time in nature, and for others: exercise, volunteering, creating art, friends, a movie, a book, going to the beach or anything else. Any experience that enables us to take a breath of fresh air from life, to relieve our confrontation with reality and charge us with positive energy—that is our emotional shelter.

Every one of us is tasked with the responsibility of identifying our own emotional shelter, since this is an amazing tool to help us, an anchor for dealing with the challenges of life and sometimes an unwanted reality (of course, do not choose an emotional shelter that poses danger, like drugs, alcohol, cults, etc..)

\*\*\*

Remember: There is nothing wrong with escaping reality from time to time. We all do this in different ways. Even reading a book, going on vacation alone and shutting off  our phone for a few hours, can air out one's mind.

# CHAPTER 47

# Physical Maintenance Alongside Emotional Maintenance

**Many studies from recent years, confirm the hypothesis that emotional stress and tension greatly increase the risk of cancer, heart disease, digestion-related diseases, skin diseases, and many other illnesses. Meaning, there is a strong connection between body and mind.**

*The German philosopher Arthur Schopenhauer said about this: "Nine-tenths of our happiness depends on our health alone." And Mahatma Gandhi, the spiritual and political Indian leader said: "It is health that is real wealth, not pieces of gold and silver."*

This fact fits in well with the main message found throughout my writings. A person, in many ways, has the power to influence their body and their health. They have the ability to prevent diseases and other troubles if they take personal responsibility for their conduct and consciousness. A person must make sure to have proper nutrition, exercise, and take the appropriate measures to reduce stress and tension. They must listen to their body and not neglect themselves physically and emotionally.

\*\*\*

The physical maintenance of one's body, together with constant emotional maintenance, will greatly increase a person's lifespan, good health and quality of life.

# CHAPTER 48

## Living in Awareness of Our Life Purpose

**In all religions and spiritual teachings there is this basic view that there is a purpose to our lives, and that it is the essence of our existence and our beings. Evolutionary processes have placed us in the "human" category, the cycle of reproduction, birth, life, death—and there is a deep motive for our existence.**

The universe operates under clear laws of nature and morality. In nature, there is a constant, circuitous flow as part of a complex and cosmic process, whose secrets are hidden from us. In every one of us is a divine spark and a destiny we must fulfill in our lifetime. We are required to find within us our most superb qualities and give to ourselves and of ourselves to the society we live in, to our environment and to the universe.

*The philosopher Friedrich Nietzsche phrased it in this sentence: "He who has a why to live for can bear almost any how.."*

It is important that every once in a while, a person ask themselves questions that most of us call "philosophical:"

**We should ask ourselves fundamental, existential questions that are relevant to our lives:**
What is the purpose of our lives? Is our physical life and physical survival the sole purpose for which we came into this world? Or is there another purpose, beneath the surface?

**We should ask ourselves about our daily conduct:**
Are our actions directed by our passions, talents and desires? Do they mostly exist based on financial, familial and social constraints? Or perhaps they exist due to the fact that we adjust our lives according to society's expectations or our family's expectations?

The American writer Henry Miller said: "Every man has his own destiny: the only imperative is to follow it, to accept it, no matter where it leads him." (from a 1956 interview between Henry Miller and his friend Ben Grauer, available on YouTube).

Making an authentic choice about our personal and professional paths in life, is the key to our happiness and self-fulfillment. This does not guarantee that our lives will be devoid of challenges and difficulties, but our ability to deal with them successfully and optimistically will be much greater than those who ride the waves of life and do not follow their hearts.

To this, some people would rightfully reply: "But our lives are a set of financial and familial constraints, and a person's first priority is to provide for their family." This is true, but it is important that we remember that work is not enslavement. Enslavement is an emotional state, not a physical one. Work, on the other hand, is supposed to provide a person with an income by utilizing their abilities and skills, and it is natural to expect that work should give one a sense of self-actualization and satisfaction. The moment work causes someone suffering, they had better look for another source of income.

We did not come into this world to suffer. Emotional distress and tension caused by the workplace may cause physical and mental illness. It is best to arrive at conclusions early on and look for another source of income.

*＊＊*

Do not wait for your body or psychological state to dictate the need to stop and change directions. Take responsibility and control of your life. Identify your weaknesses in life—the places, people and situations that weaken you—take initiative and make a change. Not as a result of necessity, but out of choice and control, out of a position of power that will allow you to build a renewable course for life with momentum and enthusiasm.

# CHAPTER 49

# A Delicate Balance

**Many of us mistakenly think that if we spend most of our energies in one field, we will succeed in it. But the truth is, the secret to a good life, according to all the spiritual guides, is the balance we create in our lives.**

*This is what Maimonides, the great Jewish scholar, physician and philosopher, wrote: "The straight path: This [involves discovering] the midpoint temperament of each and every trait that man possesses [within his personality.] This refers to the trait which is equidistant from either of the extremes, without being close to either of them. Therefore, the early Sages instructed a man to evaluate his traits, to calculate them and to direct them along the middle path, so that he will be sound {of body}."*

Meaning, the right balance and midpoint temperament are the key for a happy and stable life, a successful and serene life.

Many people do not understand that focusing exclusively on one topic, leads to neglect of other, no less important ones. For example, a person who gives his all at work but neglects his family, will pay a heavy price and will not necessarily reach his desired success. His family life will obviously deteriorate. His wife will feel neglected and so will his children.

His conduct will send them the message that they are not as important to him as his work. He takes his family for granted; they are there anyway. But he is wrong. Turning your back on your family can boomerang. He will lose his intimate relationship with his children and miss pieces of their lives that he will never get back. His partner may ignore him and their relationship will dwindle until it starves.

Once again let's see what Maimonides wrote about this: "Our Sages commanded that a man honor his wife more than his own person, and love her as he loves his own person. If he has financial resources, he should offer her benefits in accordance with his resources. He should not cast a superfluous measure of fear over her. He should talk with her gently, being neither sad nor angry."

Complete focus on one's profession will lead to exhaustion of one's cognitive abilities and vitality. If a person does not make time for contemplation and rejuvenation, the quality of their work will increasingly decline.

Moreover, a person who is not emotionally and mentally open to fields other than their profession, will find themselves years down the line without the ability to have a conversation with people, to experience awe and be excited by art, nature, literature and all other fields the world has to offer. Their cognitive abilities will gradually be damaged, since they are limiting them to just one area.

When a person operates from the standpoint of "I have no choice," and continues to work in an obsessive and compulsive manner, they send a message of weakness to their family and their social and professional surroundings. They will feel, quite often, that they have no control over their life and that life is controlling them. They will also pay for it with their health. The constant stress and troubling thoughts are bound to cause a deterioration of their physical health.

It is in times of stress and the sense of loss of control when it is most important to take a day or a few days to rejuvenate. This break will no doubt lead to new ways of thinking, an original way of problem-solving, to organizing one's thoughts about professional and personal priorities and to the changes one wishes to make in life.

One of the ways to keep a balanced life and a healthy psyche is doing physical exercise. Maimonides wrote about this: "A person must regularly move all organs of his body. The superior kind of exercise is one where the exertion of the body awakens the spirit as well. Since the joy and vitality of the spirit is what heals the body, and many have recovered from their illnesses thanks to joy of the spirit alone." Maimonides summarizes his philosophy for a balanced and healthy life: "Neutralize one's anger, balance one's eating, and increase one's movement."

\*\*\*

It is important to find in the various challenges of everyday life, a way to keep our ship of life balanced, even if the waves are high. Turning the ship to one direction will cause it to capsize. It is important to invest energy and effort in all sides of the metaphorical ship, so it can sail in a balanced and safe way and move forward.

# SECTION 7

## A JOURNEY THROUGH TIME

# CHAPTER 50

# Age is Just a Number

**When I was a young teacher, I had a conversation with a teacher who took her retirement that left a strong impression in my heart. The teacher, who was vivacious and vigorous, told me once in a candid moment: "When you get old, only your body gets old. The soul always remains young."**

This supposed innocent sentence has been well engraved in my memory and I recite it to myself daily. At every age and every period, a person must see themselves as if they are just beginning their life. This way, they will be filled with optimism, vitality, and the will to make the most of life. A person lacking a basic enthusiasm for life, who executes the tasks of life in a technical manner—is not really living. They physically exist, but their spirit, heart and emotions do not partake in their actions. Due to this, they lack vitality, enthusiasm and joy.

*American politician and writer, Benjamin Franklin said: "Some people die at age 25 and aren't buried until they are 75."* And indeed, we all know young people who, for some reason always look older than they are. Their expression is serious and their whole being emanates fatigue, lack of vitality and personal withering.

Contrary to them, we know people who are ageless. Those who have most of their lives behind them, but are full of vitality and "Joie de Vivre." Some of them are busy with different activities, others are working with full force, learning and growing, from time to time discovering a new professional direction and new interests, traveling the world, consuming culture and actively pursuing hobbies, and taking advantage of every moment of their lives with excitement and joy.

This shows us that biological age has no influence on a person's joy and vitality (assuming they are in good health). When the spirit is tired and old, it probably belongs to a person who has neglected their soul for many years until it reached the point of exhaustion and withering.

So what must we do in order to keep our mental age young and vibrant?

- First of all, we must know that the responsibility is ours alone. The choice to see life in an optimistic way, focusing on "what is" and magnifying it, is what guarantees us having a life of joy and vitality, and eventually, will shape and benefit our quality of life.

As David Ben-Gurion, Israel's first prime minister, said: "So long as a person is alive—they can change." (from a speech he delivered in 1936)

At every age it is best to keep busy with activities that enrich us emotionally and charge us with positive energy. Regular exercise that is suitable for the person, contributes to their mental and emotional well-being and fortifies their health; much has been said about the importance of physical exercise for proper blood flow in the body and proper functioning of the body's systems. At every age, physical exercise should be matched appropriately to one's physical abilities and one must choose an exercise that is enjoyable. This activity contributes also to maintaining our mental abilities, as declared by US president, John F. Kennedy: *"Physical fitness is not only one of the most important keys to a healthy body, it is the basis of dynamic and creative intellectual activity."*

- No doubt that a positive outlook on life—seeing the glass half full—determines our quality of life. A person who constantly feels as though life is not smiling at them will indeed live in a hard and tiresome reality; they will often find themselves sinking into a depression and their health will be harmed over the years due to the emotional tension and feelings of stress and pressure. We must utilize our personal happiness to the fullest in the given reality of our lives. We must live the lives we have, and not the ones we could have had.

*The Dalai Lama said: "There are only two days in the year that nothing can be done. One is called Yesterday and the other is called Tomorrow. Today is the right day to Love, Believe, Do and mostly Live."*

- Human connection with our environment has great importance, at any age. Research shows that older people who have a supportive social network are happier and healthier than those who lack this. And in any case, many people tend to neglect their social life due to pressures at work, familial obligations, or fatigue and lack of will to invest in social connections. Having regular contact with people through different interactions (classes, social gatherings, volunteering) will preserve the social aspects of our lives that are so essential to our spirits.

*Regarding this, it is recommended not to make do with only our relationships with our grown children. Each one of them has a life of their own, and we must allow them the freedom to live their lives without burdening them and relying on them to fulfill their parents' social needs.*

If so:

**Look for reasons to laugh and be joyful.** Joy strengthens the immune system of the body and our physical and mental health.

**Make a daily gratitude habit** for all that you have. Be thankful for your health, your life, your home, your income, your children, your friends, the sea, the universe, the beauty of nature and so on. These words of gratitude that you say to yourself and to the universe will enrich your spirits.

**Make a habit of thanking** the people who provide you with services. Try to see them as subjects and not objects. This may sound obvious, but let's be honest, how many of us actually make the effort of exchanging a few sentences with the exhausted person behind the checkout counter at the supermarket?

\*\*\*

Charging our emotional batteries daily, as part of an essential routine, will make our lives happier and healthier.

# CHAPTER 51

# Reconnecting with Our Inner Child

**Let us see for a moment the image of a smiling child: the child is reveling in the little details of their life. They are enjoying the simple and so-called obvious pleasures: food, a game, a hug, a song. They are living in the here and now, disregarding the time dimensions of past or future.**

At any given moment, the child, whoever they may be, enjoys "what is" in life and what the world has to offer them. They do not yet have a wider perspective of the world and all its temptations and physical and spiritual abundance. They are filled with curiosity and creativity, they are not tied to stereotypical thought patterns, and so their range of thought is open and limitless. They experience the joy of discovery each time anew, and are amazed over and over by the beauty of nature and the objects they discover in their surroundings.

In childhood, a child is not aware of the complexities of the world, of its challenges and difficulties. They are free of cynicism and criticism, and of any kind of pressures (assuming of course, they are experiencing a normal childhood).

Let us return, in certain parts of our spirits and lives, to that little child hidden within us. Let us rediscover the joy of life, creativity, the joy of discovery, and derive pleasure from the little things, from the trifles so taken for granted by adults. Let us enjoy the beauty of nature, music and marvels of the universe, and stop taking them for granted in our lives.

Lucia Capacchione, author of the book "Recovery of Your Inner Child," claims in her book that within each one of us is an inner child who holds our creative powers, and is responsible for our physical and emotional health. (From "Recovery of Your Inner Child," Touchstone publishing, 1991).

Too many people live their lives as though a millstone is placed on their necks. Instead, let us imagine that we are light, physically and emotionally, and are free of all types of stones. It is important to know that these stones are imaginary. They are artificial shackles that we placed on our own necks throughout life. Let us imagine that the whole world is available to us, and the universe is full of options and paths for us to take. We shall take what the world has to offer us.

***

We must keep our distance from anything that causes us distress and sadness, from anything that robs us of energies of liveliness and joy. It is important to know—changes and rejuvenation have no age. Just as British author and poet, George Eliot wrote: "It is never too late to be what you might have been."

# CHAPTER 52

## Less is More

**One of the ways to renew ourselves and turn over a new leaf in life, is by physically cleaning out our drawers, closets, desks, work files, work environment and life environment.**

All those storage spaces are the reflections of our soul. There we have stored our previous lives, our memories, troubles, periods we would like to remember and those we would prefer to forget. We should keep the pleasant memories, since they have within them positive and growth-inspiring energies, and the others we should pass on.

We recently moved homes. The amount of objects we had stored in the drawers of our house and all around made me feel suffocated. I felt that the mass of superfluous objects was depriving me of oxygen, breath, progress. I gave away most of the items in my old home. I wanted to enter a new home free and clear of heavy burdens from previous times in my life. Suddenly I felt a relief, in body and in spirit. I reached the conclusion that we must invest in the experiences of life and not in things. The experiences are what shape our identities and our sense of joy and happiness. The objects will remain in the drawers like a stone that cannot be overturned.

A person who is at a crossroad, in darkness, in confusion, in deliberation with themselves about their path in life—must first of all organize the files and drawers of their life. They must throw out all that is unnecessary and keep only what they use daily. Also functioning objects that have no use should be donated to those who need them. Less is more. Think about it.

By sorting and cleaning we will purify our lives from influences and shadows of the past and be cleansed of negative energies. In this way, we open a new channel in our lives. We allow new energies to enter and flow into our lives. We open blockages in our lives. Old objects that have no use block our lives from renewal.

Other methods of rejuvenation include buying new clothes, giving away old clothes to people who would be happy to have them, and buying nice items and tools for your home. You can touch up the walls, repaint, move furniture around, hang a new picture, launder the curtains, do some light renovations. As for external rejuvenation, we can change our hairstyles, change perfumes, color our hair, take up a new class, read a spiritual book, light candles.

***

I once read that according to the art of feng shui, a home must have hanging in it a picture of flowing water: a river, waterfall, fountain— preferably on the northern side of the house. Do as you see fit. As long as you feel renewal in your lives.

# CHAPTER 53

# Where is Everyone Rushing to?

**When I look around me, I find that almost all people are in a hurry. Everyone lives with the sense that they have somewhere they need to get to. The rat-race of life pulls them in a thousand directions with a further thousand tasks to be done, and everyone feels as though they are a minute behind on their next assignment.**

Our personal "Task Train" is in constant motion and does not stop for a moment. We feel that if we simply hurry up a little, then later when we achieve our goals, our lives will be calmer and more peaceful. We live under the illusion that the pressure is temporary, that in a little while it will pass and we will arrive at that place of silence, calmness and serenity we so long for.

If a photographer were to document the human condition from the outside, we would see an image of anxious and nervous people, who are wholly focused on their next assignment and are missing the wonderful world around them. When we are tuned in with our whole being, physically and emotionally to a task at hand, we forget to look around. We do not see other people. We are disconnected from them and feel estranged from them and from ourselves. The beauty of the world becomes transparent to us, we do not notice the emotional distress of those around us, and so on. Our intention of withstanding the pressure of our tasks and assignments prevents us from enjoying our lives in the present and living them to the fullest. Most of us live feeling that the present period is the journal of our lives while the real movie has yet to begin.

Let us put the cards on the table. The (metaphorical) "movie" started long ago, and not only that, it sometimes ends rather abruptly. The optimists among us will say that we are currently in the middle of the movie, and if we do not start right now, relaxing in our lives and experiencing them to their fullest—it will never happen.

*The politician William Penn, founder of the American Province of Pennsylvania, said: "Time is what we want most and what we use worst."*

The painful awakening usually occurs at a time of crisis, a personal or health-related crisis. Unfortunately, people wake up from the illusion of "journal time" only when they experience a difficult trauma such as a disease or a disaster. Only then do they realize that there is no point to the crazy rat-race of their lives, which contributes nothing to success.

Moreover, people who rush from one task to the next, cannot delve into it deeply and give it the appropriate amount of time and thought, and in the end, will not execute it in a thorough way. Additionally, at times they might need to return to that same project because it was not completed properly, and so they will lose valuable time for nothing. Executing tasks in a superficial, unprofessional way, harms a person's professional credibility, their integrity and their image in society as well as their own self-image. It is true what they say: when you try to do everything, you end up with nothing. When the quality of your work is examined, it isn't relevant how many tasks you were doing simultaneously, but how professional and thorough your work is. And so, you had better invest your maximum time and energy in it, without pressure.

If we are wise enough to pause the race from time to time, to slow down the rhythm of our lives, we will improve our performance immeasurably in different areas. Also, our relationships will improve immeasurably. Personal connections will take place in a calm manner and out of genuine interest in the other person.

Some of us sin by calculating in our minds, while listening to another person, how much precious time they are robbing from us. When we are speaking with a person, but are constantly thinking about our next task, it is likely that we will not really be able to identify and show them true empathy. We must disconnect from our troubling thoughts and focus our attention on the person in front of us. Relationships should come from a deep, authentic place and not from a social commitment. From a place of true interest and caring, and not to check something off our to-do list.

The concept of relationships includes in it also our attitude toward the people closest to us. Usually, they are the first to pay the price of our crazy life race. But it is them, above all, who are worthy of receiving our full attention and emotional effort. Many parents discover too late in their lives that they have missed having a deep relationship with their children, but at their older age it is much harder to bridge the gap.

A calm person, one who emanates ease and control, has a higher chance of reaching senior ranks and professional and personal successes in life. They exude confidence in themselves and in the processes they command. The process of them becoming exhausted and physically and mentally fatigued will be slower, their health will be improved and they will have a better quality of life.

For most people, time is the most valuable resource. We are all trying to fill it as much as possible with activities and tasks, obligations and leisure activities, work and much more. We are tormented with thoughts about how we have not managed to do everything we set out to do due to a lack of time. We get upset when we are stuck in traffic, or standing in line at the bank, are held back at the doctor's office, at governmental departments and so on. How much energy and anger do we invest in racing after lost time…. This never-ending chase after time drains us physically and emotionally.

It is important to know: if we hurry, there is no guarantee that we will be more successful in life. The opposite. It has been said: "Haste makes waste." Try and imagine how many accidents could have been prevented and how many lives could have been saved if we hurried less on the roads.

Life is conducted according to its own rules, the laws of the universe. They have a calm and serene rhythm, just as Earth revolves in a steady, monotonous and unified rhythm. I suggest we try and match the rhythm of our lives to the rhythm of the universe.

- Let us stop rushing and act with calmness. In this way we will make fewer mistakes and will not have to spend time correcting them.

- Let us be extra careful, and we will not have to stop our lives due to an accident.
- Let us learn to listen to each other, and the society we live in will be less violent and tense.
- Let us enjoy every moment in life, experience it with pleasure, and without feeling pressure to move on to the next task.
- Let us learn to listen to a friend in need. We must never think of it, under any circumstances, as a waste of time, even if we have a thousand tasks to complete. If we dedicate our full attention to this person in their time of need, they will return the favor when we are in need of empathy, support and a listening ear.

Utilitarian people, who only do what is practical, will pay for this in one way or another. Eventually, everything balances out in life, and a person must be able to answer for their actions and conduct in life. In the "register of life," we pay for everything in the end, and everything we do comes back to us. If we give to others of ourselves, they and the universe will return the favor in kind. This is the law of the universe. Giving begets giving and vice versa.

It is just as important that we dedicate time to ourselves. For vacation, for rejuvenation, for thought and for time alone. Quality time with ourselves will give us renewed energy to experience life powerfully and with great pleasure.

*John Wanamaker, the American entrepreneur, once said: "People who cannot find time for recreation are obliged sooner or later to find time for illness."*

\*\*\*

Let us decide, in this moment, that there is no need to wait for tomorrow to start a new life. We can start the process now. A wise person once said, "If you persistently walk in the same way, it is likely you will end up in the same place." Let's stop, close our eyes, take a deep breath and begin our new lives. Let's walk a bit slower...

# CHAPTER 54

# No Excuses!

**Many people use life's challenges and tasks as an excuse for not making changes, for avoiding developing their hobbies, for lack of initiative and for passivity. The statement "I'm pressed for time" is our most commonly used sentence.**

*The Chinese philosopher Confucius described time with these words: "Time flows away like the water in the river, day and night they flow incessantly."*

Each one of us lives in our own bubble. We are all busy with the chores of life. Let us picture it as millions of tiny bubbles with millions of people in them running around breathless from place to place. Everybody is making a living, fulfilling their obligations to their homes and families, and feeling troubled with bureaucratic matters of this kind or that. All humans on earth deal with surprisingly similar problems: career, love, children, money, health and more.

All these can be seen as obvious challenges of life. The foundation of a healthy life on earth. Life itself is made up of tasks, they are the DNA of life. We must accept it as fact, that as long as we are living and breathing, there will always be more assignments to carry out and more challenges to deal with. However, we must not let these tasks blind us from seeing our true needs. Our children will need us at every age, and so will our parents. The work will always claim what it deserves.

And within the abundance of these tasks—we must not lose our "self" and what really matters to us: what we love doing, and who we love being around. What causes us joy and pleasure and what causes the opposite. We must be able to answer these questions for ourselves, if only so that we may change our routines even in the slightest, improve them and our emotional well-being.

*Spanish author and satirist Baltasar Gracian viewed planning our time as a necessary condition for enjoying life: "Knowing how to divide our time appropriately is knowing how to enjoy life."*

*Chinese philosopher Lao Tzu said about this: "Time is a created thing. To say I don't have time is like saying, I don't want to."*

*And French writer and publicist Jean de La Bruyère claimed that "Those who make the worst use of their time are the first to complain of its brevity."*

\*\*\*

We must honestly examine what are the most important things to us in life. This kind of exploration demands that we sometimes sit alone with ourselves, in reflective observation, and connect with our inner selves. Don't worry, this will only do us good!

# CHAPTER 55

## Take it Slow

**Sometimes I reflect on the will of my beloved grandmother, Eva Zalmanovich, of blessed memory, and tears come to my eyes. My elderly grandmother, who survived two world wars and the wars of the State of Israel, who lost a wonderful partner and a beloved son who was only 43 years old when he died (my father, Ofer, of blessed memory), taught me a valuable lesson. She asked that her descendants live long and joyful lives.**

My grandmother had great life wisdom and was very modest. All the days of her life, until age 99, she kept her dignity and never let a word of gossip slip out of her mouth. I learned from her a useful lesson: all about having love for life, love for people and great love for family.

The most important message I learned from her was to make the most out of any situation a person is in. To see the good and positive in every situation and be happy for it.

*As Theodore Roosevelt, the 26th US president said: "Do what you can with what you have, where you are."*

Often we all feel as though the world around us is too fast, too cruel, too cynical and hard, too demanding, lacking forgiveness and compassion. We must know that in the reality of life, we must be forgiving of ourselves; must be full of compassion, love and self-forgiveness. We must adopt a technique for life in a "protective bubble," which means surrounding ourselves with an invisible shield that will not allow the pressures of life to harm us. We have no way of controlling reality. It will often behave very differently than we would expect. However, we must not torment ourselves. We must accept this as a fact. We must know that this is how things are and they are not under our control, and in this reality we must protect our basic happiness, reach peace of mind and the maximal fulfillment of our potential.

*The great Chinese philosopher Confucius said: "Good people strengthen themselves ceaselessly."*

If we develop defense mechanisms and allow our spirit to remain calm, if we learn not to get stressed, upset, angry or hurt, then we will emanate outwards our feelings of calmness and personal confidence. Our peace of mind will reflect unto our surroundings, and will naturally influence it for the better.

*John Newton, Anglican cleric and abolitionist, wrote: "We can easily manage if we will only take, each day, the burden appointed to it. But the load will be too heavy for us if we carry yesterday's burden over again today, and then add the burden of the morrow before we are required to bear it."*

If we tell ourselves that "the system" (and it does not matter where: work, governmental departments, national insurance, university, the bank, the army, in an organization etc..) does not see us at all as individuals but as part of a greater team, and that the systems of life are conducted in a bureaucratic manner with no regard for the private person—then we will know how to protect ourselves from it. We will know to apply mental defenses so as not to be harmed or weakened.

How can we do this?

- First of all, I would suggest that we all slow down the pace of life. Let us walk slower and do everything while meticulously caring for the smallest details. Let us do everything slowly, even if that means we will do less.

- Just as importantly, we must not give up on our basic human needs, one of which is the ability to think clearly. A person who is racing against the clock their whole lives, loses their social and human sensitivity along the way. They miss out on great opportunities, become blind to what is happening around them, and stop listening to themselves and to others. Hurried people do things in a mechanical way and they lose connection with their emotions and soul. They may forget important and significant details, and for that they will often fail their missions.

- Let us imagine ourselves as pilots looking at our lives from above. The ability to create distance from events we are a part of and observe life from "high up," saves us many times from unnecessary emotional involvement and mental stress, things which harm the regular execution of tasks in our lives. Viewing things from above will give us a sense of control over our lives, like the glory of a king who rules his life.

*The spiritual teacher and author Carl Honoré says: "Slower, it turns out, often means better—better health, better work, better business, better family life, better exercise, better cuisine and better sex." (TED talk of Carl Honoré "In Praise of Slowness. https://www.ted.com/talks/ carl_honore_in_praise_of_slowness)*

*And Confucius said: "It does not matter how slowly you go as long as you do not stop." Think about it.*

***

Let us memorize: From now on let's stop thinking about how to change the framework in which we live. Rather, let's think about how to make the most out of it for our needs.

# CHAPTER 56

# Emotional Serenity

**Every person strives to reach that serene time of their lives. The word serenity means comfortable physical conditions, obviously, a job that is suitable in effort for the age of the person, a warm and comforting home, a loving and kind relationship, economic well-being that provides a sense of security and calm.**

However, it is emotional serenity that is so crucial. This is the time of life when a person makes peace with who they are, no matter their strengths or limitations. They stop examining themselves with a magnifying glass regarding every single move, regarding how they speak and act, and stop blaming themselves for past or present failures. The person accepts and loves themselves just as they are.

*The author and journalist Oscar Wilde said: "To love oneself is the beginning of a lifelong romance."*

And don't make light of this. Most people are busy throughout their lives with self-flagellation, frustration, and blaming themselves and others. Once a person begins loving themselves as they are and forgiving themselves—their reality will change and they will reach a level of emotional peace and self-acceptance.

*Louise Hay, The American author who wrote many self-help books and developed a self-healing method using positive thinking, said about this: "Remember, you have been criticizing yourself for years and it hasn't worked. Try approving of yourself and see what happens."* (YouTube video "How Thoughts Create Reality" https://www.youtube.com/watch?v=yuPtq8_c3II)

This stage usually arrives through the understanding that life can be over in an instant. Sometimes, following a life-changing event that changes one's worldview. At once, the person realizes that the sand is quickly running out of their life's hourglass, that life is only lived once. The understanding reaches into their consciousness that there is no absolute truth, and so every person must live according to their truth and with self-love. That is where lies the potential for happiness, self-fulfillment, and emotional serenity.

- Emotional serenity means disconnecting from people who make us feel guilty, frustrated, or emotional pain, for whatever reason.
- Emotional serenity means doing what I love, without caring for emotional manipulations placed on me by my surroundings.
- Emotional serenity means living without guilt feelings and without thinking automatically about what "I should," but about what "I want."
- Emotional serenity means living according to what is good for me and right for me.
- Emotional serenity means letting go of the need to receive external approval from my surroundings, and of the need to be liked and prove how "good" I am.
- Emotional serenity means living by "The book of my soul" and not "The book of social requirements."

- Emotional serenity means living life by the natural flow, with ease, without overload and unnecessary difficulty. It means shedding our fears, blocks, hindrances, concerns and stresses.
- Emotional serenity means letting go of the need to provide explanations to our parents, our children, our friends, to the people we like and to those we don't like.
- Emotional serenity means also loving the people around us. Just as we do not want to be emotionally manipulated, through guilt or anger, we must not do this to others.

*The Chinese philosopher Lao Tzu wrote 2300 years ago: "Men are born soft and supple; dead they are stiff and hard. Plants are born tender and pliant; dead, they are brittle and dry. Thus, whoever is stiff and inflexible is a disciple of death. Whoever is soft and yielding is a disciple of life. The hard and stiff will be broken. The soft and supple will prevail."*

There are people for whom simple tasks, such as hosting family, shopping and cooking, are experienced as highly stressful tasks that rob them of emotional energy. Their thoughts about the necessary preparations, the effort, the mess, the noise, the tiredness, create emotional stress that overpowers their ability to enjoy the situation. This is not due to the effort itself, but the emotional effort involved. The aspiration for "perfection" neutralizes in advance any chance at enjoying the event.

The moment we let go of the desire to be perfect, we will start enjoying the smaller moments of our lives. We will derive pleasure from the simple mundane tasks, big or small. Once the fear of failure isn't breathing down our necks, we can be free to focus on carrying out our daily tasks with pleasure, enjoyment and with the full force of our abilities and emotions. When we live our lives with a sense of freedom and release from criticism and judgment from others, it is likely we will feel serene and happy. With that, we must be real and honest with those around us. We must be honest about our desires, our wishes and our pain, so that the environment can treat us accordingly.

*Just as Brigham Yang, former leader of The Church of Jesus Christ of Latter-day Saints, wrote: "Why should we worry about what others think of us, do we have more confidence in their opinions than we do our own?"*

*François de La Rochefoucauld, French author and satirist, said: "It is easier to be wise for others than for ourselves."*

*And Mother Teresa, the humanitarian activist and Nobel Peace Prize winner, said: "If you judge people, you have no time to love them."*

Let us remember: We will often find people in our environment who take from us emotionally, those who do not wish us success, and they may weaken us with their criticism, cynicism and ridicule. Once we identify this "criticism" as malice, evil and jealousy, we must learn to ignore it and not let it penetrate our layer of emotional serenity.

# SECTION 8

## THE POWER OF WORDS

# CHAPTER 57

# Life and Death Are in the Power of the Tongue

**Our sages have said that "Life and death are in the power of the tongue," and indeed words have an immense energetic influence on our thoughts, lives, successes or failures, reality, and our relationships with the world around us.**

Let us start seeing words as a tool to strengthen ourselves and others. Let's avoid using negative words that attract negative energy, and use positive words that attract positive energy. Words create reality according to our choices.

It is important to be strict about the way we speak and the contents of our words. We must carefully choose our words when we are asked to criticize, so our words will achieve a positive result. Violent words will not contribute to anything, they will only achieve the opposite. Positive words, however, will enable us to live in harmony with our surroundings, even if it is not a supportive one. Positive words will help us gain supporters for our ideas, plans and projects we wish to execute. Positive words will encourage us to move on in spite of our failures.

*The philosopher Baruch Spinoza said: "Words give thought their highest and noblest existence."*

*Roman poet and philosopher Horace, who lived in the first century BC, said: "A word once uttered can never be recalled."*

*And Maimonides said: "Think and consider your words before uttering them, for you will not be able to take them back." (from "Iggeret Hamusar")*

It is best to keep our distance from those who gossip, who spread negative words about others and express negative ideas. This type of talk usually expresses feelings of frustration, anger, jealousy, envy, maliciousness and evilness, and they emanate negative energy.

*Honoré de Balzac, the French novelist and playwright, demonstrated the negative power of words in the sentence: "There are words which cut like steel."*

It is important that we know that people who use negative words attract to them negative energy and like-minded people, and their environment in life will be loaded with negative energy. Contrary to them, people who view the word with love and compassion will use positive, forgiving and softened words, both toward themselves and those around them, and will attract to them positive energy.

There is a law in nature and the universe: "Like attracts like." So positive is attracted to positive, creates a circle of positive people around it and brings positive results that influence all areas of life.

Because of this, we must learn to choose words that are hopeful and not ones that describe terminal and negative situations. So, for example, instead of the word "difficulties" we will say "challenges," and instead of "a terrible, horrible situation" we will say, "a complicated situation that requires great effort." Instead of "I'm feeling despair," we will say, "I'm not in such a good mood," and instead of the definitions "causing despair" or "catastrophe," we must try and say, "yes, the situation is difficult, but let us think together how we can handle this challenge."

Do not emanate or use words that describe endings, lack of purpose, lack of hope. Try to always choose words that describe a momentary state of lack of success, those which still hold the possibility for future success. This will open a symbolic, energetic window for future success in whatever you failed this time around.

Use encouraging words toward yourself and others. Instead of saying "I'm a total loser at math and there's no way I'll succeed," say "Math and I don't really get along. I guess I still haven't found the teacher who will help me succeed," or "It's possible I haven't put in enough of an effort to succeed."

Remember: It is always possible to fix something, to try again, to improve, to learn new things. Never shut down the conversation and don't "eulogize" others—and certainly not yourselves. Use softer words to describe failure. Instead of failure, say "unsuccessful" or, "This time it didn't work," and keep trying new ways of dealing with the challenge.

*A Japanese proverb says: "One word is enough to cause many troubles."*

Words have an incredible power to build—both yourself and others. Just as with one sentence you can help others and empower them (and certainly also yourselves), words also have an incredibly destructive power. Whoever is capable of trampling someone with words, is capable of physically trampling someone, as the Jewish German poet Heinrich Heine said: "Where they burn books, they will also ultimately burn people." A sentence that chillingly turned out to be true in 1933, when the Nazis in Germany began burning books that expressed the spirit of freedom, democracy and equality of mankind.

Because indeed, burning words is burning ideas. Words have a tremendous power to influence people and cause revolutions. Words create a national ethos. They are capable of recruiting people to an idea to the point of sacrificing their lives for it.

*A Greek proverb says: "A word at the wrong time, corrupts a man's life."*

We must mean our words not merely when speaking them, but also in writing. Especially in this age of technology—which is the age of written communication (e-mails, WhatsApp, Twitter, Facebook, instant messages)—we should adopt a respectful writing habit, one which uses words of cooperation and joint thinking.

In order to succeed in complex political work, the written word is very important. Most workplaces are actually political arenas, and so, every e-mail must be carefully thought out and not spontaneous. Using the right words—not harsh, not extreme, words that do not carry any blame or insult but the opposite—will allow you to live peacefully and succeed in a competitive workplace. If you emanate positive energy through your words, you can recruit supporters to execute the projects you wish to produce.

***

Start seeing words as a means to attract positive energy into your life and to create a positive reality of your choosing.

# CHAPTER 58

# Five Important Little Words

**Courage, responsibility, self-belief, love and truth. All of these will be our guiding lights in life.**

### Courage

In order to live life to the fullest, with pleasure and self-realization, a person must show courage and valor and live while overcoming fears and concerns. It's true, fear is a natural feeling, but we must adopt ways of overcoming it, otherwise it will manage our lives and determine our decisions for us in the crossroads of life.

Fear will block thousands of paths and avenues that we might take to fulfill our dreams. Courage will allow us to try the variety of possibilities that are open to us.

Nelson Mandela, former president of South Africa, "father of the nation," said in his inaugural speech in 1994: "Our deepest fear is not that we are inadequate. Our deepest fear is that we are powerful beyond measure. It is our light, not our darkness, that most frightens us. We ask ourselves, 'Who am I to be brilliant, gorgeous, talented and fabulous?' Actually, who are you not to be? As we let our own light shine, we unconsciously give other people our permission to do the same. As we are liberated from our own fear, our presence automatically liberates others."

## Responsibility

In any path we take, personally and professionally, we must show personal responsibility, consideration and willingness to take responsibility for the consequences of our actions. It is the expression of our inner truth and integrity, fairness and decency.

## Self-belief

Believing in ourselves is the most important thing. But at the same time, we must also believe in others, since our lives blend and weave with the lives of others. Realizing our dreams involves cooperating with other people and so we must trust them. For this we must choose the most honest, industrious and committed people, so they will walk with us on the path we choose.

It is important that we first of all believe in ourselves; that we have the ability to initiate processes, to grow and promote ourselves and society. And so we must begin to become aware of our immense innate powers. Concurrently, we must believe that the universe is behind us, supporting us and assisting us to synchronize our goals and aspirations with the cosmic reality.

Ze'ev Jabotinsky, Russian Jewish Revisionist Zionist leader, said: "Man is incapable of uprooting from his heart the hope for a better future." Believe that you have the ability to create the reality that you seek for your life.

## Love

First and foremost, we must look at the world from a loving and compassionate point of view. Criticizing our environment is legitimate, but it is best if that is not the starting point of our attitude toward life. It is a negative starting point that focuses on the flaws of the world and not its positive aspects. In the concept "love" we will also include love for ourselves and love for others. The willingness to forgive ourselves and others. Empathy and the ability to listen to another person and their troubles.

## Truth

Truth is the rock of our existence, and this means we must stick to the path of honesty and morality, without the use of lies, gossip and manipulations. The path of honesty will promise that we will get far on our journey for many years, together with travel partners who will help us fulfill our dreams.

Truth, transparency and integrity in our personal, professional and business relationships, will promise us credibility. It has been said in our Jewish sources that "A good name is better than fine perfume." Remember always that whoever tries to attain goals in the short-term and cuts corners to achieve this and does not always stick to the path of honesty—will end up losing in the long run.

Stick to the righteous path, even though it is longer and harder, because it will guarantee that you will succeed in the really big things.

\*\*\*

*We shall finish with the beautiful words of Rabbi Abraham Isaac Kook: "Every person must know and understand, that inside them burns a candle, and their candle is not like that of their friend's, and there is no person without a candle. And every person must know and understand that they must toil and share the light of this candle with others, kindle it to a grand flaming torch with which to illuminate the world."*

# SECTION 9

## GENDER

## CHAPTER 59

## How Do We Perceive Ourselves?

**Gender, in short, is the traditions, social perceptions, cultural constructs and everything we carry in our consciousness from the time we are born, regarding the characteristics of men and women and their roles in society. All of these are acquired consciously and subconsciously through a process of socialization, and they influence the structure of society politically, economically, socially, culturally and every other area.**

Writer and philosopher Simone de Beauvoir, known for her feminist writings, highlights the fact that a woman's character is shaped by the messages she received from the education, the culture and the society in which she was raised. (*"The Second Sex": "One is not born, but rather becomes, a woman."* Vintage Classics Publishing, 2011)

I have been working in the field of gender for many years, in research (I have a doctorate in gender and Zionism) in activist work (as a national guide for equality between genders in the ministry of education), and through volunteering (with sexually abused women and prostitution). After many years of experience and being up close and personal, I can say with certainty that the topic of gender has a far-reaching impact on the lives of both men and women, whether they lead normal lives or are in the outskirts of society.

The way girls are raised by their parents is different than the way boys are raised, and we see the results of this in the statistics: few women in influential positions, in academia and also in economic and political positions. The reasons are complex, but the bottom line is the same: the potential of women is not being fulfilled on a personal, social and national level.

I am calling all parents to attention regarding their gender bias. Encourage your daughters the same way you encourage your sons, and send them the message that they have the ability to achieve any goal they want, with emphasis on utilizing their strengths. In many cases, parents cooperate with the agents of socialization and emphasize the importance of feminine beauty over anything else. I am not belittling feminine beauty and aesthetics, but they must not be first priority. Girls must develop their personal skills in different areas and aspire to fulfill themselves, personality-wise and talent-wise, without relying on their external looks that make them a pretty hanger and detract from them their humanity and array of skills.

As parents, encourage conversations in your home about equal partnership. A partnership where the family gains from having two parents who are professionally satisfied and compensated appropriately.

For years I led empowerment workshops for female students. To my understanding, this workshop holds revolutionary potential, since the girls receive tools for self-empowerment and a critical lens regarding social perceptions and messages about gender that are placed on them by the media and the advertising world.

It is important that teachers and parents strengthen the girls' feelings of capability (and the boys', of course, too), because the feeling of capability is more important than the capability itself. Strengthen the girls' motivation to fulfill their aspirations and realize their innate potential.

Additionally, it is important that educators speak about gender issues in class and dedicated lessons.

Unfortunately, during my years working with teachers, especially the women, I discovered that in many cases the teachers themselves have low self-esteem and a low self-image. The reasons for this are complex, some of which stem from years of being worn down by the education system and due to the fact that in many cases, their work is transparent and not compensated for. Another part of the reason is gender. According to studies, many women have a very low sense of personal capability and they belittle themselves. One of the missions I saw in front of me, was to ingrain in them a professional pride and high self-esteem for both themselves and their position. Female teachers (and the male ones, too) have every reason to lift their heads up high and feel great pride, since they hold the keys to the future of the nation and the quality of the future of humanity.

Many women give up on their careers and on fulfilling their aspirations academically and professionally due to familial obligations. However, in the end, when their children grow up, they carry the great frustration of not having fulfilled themselves. I call out to all women—do not give up on yourselves. If you have decided to dedicate several years to raising a family, it is important that this decision be made out of free will and not out of constraints. Remember that you share the children with your partner, and the responsibility for their education should be a joint one. Find the way for both of you to utilize your abilities and fulfill your aspirations. This is not a simple challenge but it is possible.

In spite of all this, in the last few decades, and especially during the last one, we are seeing a positive change in trend in the field of gender. A change in public awareness, in education, in dividing resources, and in the national statistics.

Equality between genders is a social and national interest, and not only that of women. It relieves men too from binding social perceptions. The more a society has equality between genders, the more its statistics improve, and so it is in the best interest of society as a whole.

All this being said, we must shine a spotlight on a sensitive topic that is a matter of life or death, which is sexual abuse and its tragic consequences.
It is important that parents and teachers remain alert and vigilant about the mental and emotional states of boys and girls, so that if need be, they can identify those who have been harmed. Most sexual offenses are carried out by people from their inner circle. Nowadays, in the age of the internet, the "repertoire" of offenses has widened and they are also carried out in other ways.

Following my years of experience with sexual abuse survivors, I can testify to the harsh consequences of these offenses on the rest of their lives. Almost 100 percent of women in prostitution have experienced sexual abuse as a child. It is important that we, as a society, give our full support and assistance to these survivors so they can rehabilitate themselves and lead normal lives.

***

Remember: behind the numbers and statistics are people—women and men—and they have rights: the right to happiness, freedom, self-realization and release from social and cultural bonds regarding the roles of men and women in society.

# CHAPTER 60

# The Feminine Beauty Ideal—An Obstacle

**Supposedly, today, all possibilities are open to both men and women. And yet, the discrimination against women is still ingrained in the culture, social perceptions and religions. Today, it is often hidden from plain sight, but still exists deep down in consciousness. It is very hard to uproot beliefs and social opinions—something which women themselves have internalized for generations. The beauty ideal is an essential topic worthy of raising and discussing in the conversation about gender equality.**

Here I turn to my female sisters, build your personal and professional identities on your skills and strengths as humans—in combination with hard work, determination and effort. Do not build your identity on external looks in spite of the messages you have been receiving powerfully since childhood.

*Former prime minister of Israel, Golda Meir, addressed women with this statement: "Make the most of yourself by fanning the tiny, inner sparks of possibility into flames of achievement."*

The beauty ideal is a goal in of itself, made by women themselves. From a very young age, we are taught, through open or subliminal messages, through the agents of socialization (parents, extended family, our peers, the media, commercials, movies, TV shows, books) that what is important about a woman is her beauty and external looks: her face, her thin body, her clothes, her jewelry, her makeup and so on. Behind these messages are also the global interests of huge commercial companies. The message to women is clear: You are worthy as a human if you are pretty and attractive. These codes cause millions of girls and women to experience feelings of inferiority and misery due to how they look and their body build, as well as lack of confidence, and in extreme cases, also severe phenomena like anorexia and bulimia.

*In this context, let us read the words of German playwright, poet and writer Friedrich Schiller: "The iron chain and the silken cord are both equally bonds."*

The beauty ideal erases our human value, and, in fact, delegitimizes us as humans. It dehumanizes us, discriminates and humiliates us, and it's about time we stopped cooperating with it. This social and cultural code is nothing but a means of suppressing women and objectifying them. It indirectly carries the covert message that women only have bodies, not feelings, and so they are not fit to serve in roles that are meaningful and require responsibility.

The beauty ideal also serves the hierarchy and perpetuates the patriarchal rule. It is another means of the patriarchy to control women, steer them, set their status as inferior, as equal only if they are pretty hangers. It is a trap. We all enjoy receiving compliments for our looks, but we must not base our personalities and our personal and professional identities on them.

I am not discounting nurturing one's physical appearance. This is absolutely the choice of every woman. But if you choose to do so, nurture yourselves for your good feeling only. Do not base your personal and professional progress on your appearance.

Remember: building your identity on external appearances is a shallow and superficial matter. It will lead to people treating you according to your physical appearance. They will not see you as a serious partner of leadership and decision-making (in the family, workplace, organization and any other place) or as a human that is capable of creating a meaningful conversation (political, academic, economic, artistic or social).

It is important that you develop a professional path that will provide you financial independence, and most importantly—remember that at some point in life, the charm of externalities will fade and you will not be able to rely on it anymore. And then? You will have to reinvent yourself. So, develop your skills, acquire an education, a profession, work hard and be excellent in your chosen field.

*Founder of the successful cosmetics company, Estée Lauder, said: "I didn't get there by wishing for it, or hoping for it, but by working hard."*

Indeed, it is very difficult to be free of such powerful messages that are transmitted to us from the moment we are born about our role in society and how we should look. That is why it is important to develop a critical eye and reiterate to ourselves and our daughters that their human value is not measured by their beauty, but by their qualities, by utilizing their talents and by their ability to develop their own personal and professional course that is rewarding and satisfying. It is important to speak to girls about this topic from a young age.

*Madonna: "If your joy is derived from what society thinks of you, you're always going to be disappointed."*

*Canadian model, Chantelle Brown, discovered at the age of four that she has a skin disease called vitiligo, which causes white spots to appear all over her body. Chantelle (known as Winnie Harlow), who was blessed with a rare beauty, decided to turn her disadvantage into an advantage and became a big star in the US. With courage and honesty, she shares with her fans her emotional experiences from childhood and the suffering she felt due to her being unusual. She says that during adolescence, she realized that only self-acceptance will lead to self-love and open the doors for happiness and success, and for her, spreading this message is her calling in life.*

***

This is true freedom: being yourself while freeing yourself from social constructs and cultural perceptions about what is expected of women.

# SECTION 10

## FAMILY AND RELATIONSHIPS

# CHAPTER 61

# Equal Among Equals

**An equal relationship is one that has an unwritten agreement between the couple, according to which each side has the equal opportunity to utilize their skills and strengths, professionally or academically and in any area of interest. In an equal relationship, each one gives according to their ability and skill-set, and the relationship is based on agreements and mutuality between the couple. This mutuality encourages growth and is the very potential for financial and professional prosperity both for each person individually and for the whole family unit.**

*In Ecclesiastes 4, 9, it is written: "Two are better than one, because they have a good return for their labor."*

An equal and respectful partnership is a healthy system that is free of social and cultural perceptions regarding men and women's roles, and does not impose on them any roles or require them to relinquish anything due to their gender.

*Maimonides has written about the need for mutual respect and for a man, who in his time was considered head of the family and provider, to treat his wife respectfully: "The Sages have directed us, saying:*

*One should always eat less than befits his income, dress as befits [his income], and provide for his wife and children beyond what befits [his income]."*

Meaning, a man's greatest emotional and physical investment should be in his wife and children.

An equal partnership between a couple is a system where any relinquishment made by one side is done out of free will, and neither side has additional rights because they earn more money or because they brought more assets into the relationship and so on.

When there is no negotiating within the relationship, when there is no discussion or compromise, this is a bad situation because it means there is complete control on one side, and complete lack of expression on the other side. Meaning, discrimination. In a relationship that has a hierarchy and only one side has the final say, the other side will be left frustrated and angry.

In an equal relationship the family unit is strong because both sides are developing their own course in life. This relationship is typically happy, powerful and filled with positive energy, which allows it to achieve great heights in any field.

Couples who are fulfilling themselves professionally, serve as an example of equal treatment and self-fulfillment for their children. The financial situation of the family will also improve when both partners are part of the workforce, realizing their personal abilities and contributing to the family's finances.

*Rabbi Akiva said in the Talmud: "If a man and woman merit reward through a faithful marriage, the Divine Presence rests between them. If they do not merit reward, fire consumes them." (Sotah tractate, 17,2) Meaning, a good relationship is a recipe for a happy and prosperous life, and receives the blessing of the creator.*

*The Lubavitcher Rebbe wrote the following to a hassid who asked for advice on how to deal with difficulties and arguments in a relationship: "He and his wife must each do everything they can to bring their hearts closer and strengthen peace in the home. And if they really will it—certainly they will succeed."*

And just as equality between sexes is a high priority for social and national interest, since all social statistics improve—health, education, life expectancy, reduction in violence, economic prosperity—so too on the micro level, the family level. Just as equality between sexes strengthens society in all ways, so too it strengthens the family unit in all areas: financial, professional, cultural and social.

**An equal partnership** allows each individual in the couple to push forward.

**An unequal partnership** does not allow this. It is full of power struggles, frustrations and anger, something which weakens it from the inside.

**An equal partnership** allows each person in the couple to focus on growth—economically, culturally, and socially. Agreements, compromises, and focusing on a joint goal, strengthen the family unit in all ways.

276 | D<strike>R</strike>. O<strike>RNA</strike> M<strike>ARKUS</strike> B<strike>EN</strike> Z<strike>VI</strike>

**An unequal partnership**, which consists of conflicts and fights, weakens the family unit. A system that lacks respect and equality, will be stagnant and stuck and will not be able to soar and flourish.

**An equal partnership** leads to possibilities for prosperity. Each individually, and also the family as a whole, will flourish financially. Equality leads to prosperity.

**An unequal partnership** that consists of power struggles and ego, and the attempts of each person to establish their status at home—does not leave the emotional energy for building and growing the family unit. The emotional resources are wasted on futile struggles and unnecessary heartache, and create a state of stuckness: in career, financially, as individuals and within the family unit.

The great playwright William Shakespeare said: "Love takes the meaning in love's conference. I mean, that my heart unto yours is knit so that but one heart we can make of it." (from "A Midsummer Night's Dream")

We must remember: The success of our partner is always our success as well, and vice versa. If we know this and support each other, each one of us will feel that their marriage is a safety net in their life, one that enables them to fully realize the full potential of their abilities. It is written in the Old Testament: "Therefore shall a man leave his father and his mother, and shall cleave unto his wife, and they shall be one flesh." Meaning, they become one being in intent and action.

This does not mean that a couple will live a life devoid of arguments and conflict. It is natural and understandable to have disagreements, difficulties and fights as an inseparable part of a couple's life. And yet, it is important that each couple learn to solve their problems through effective communication, with tolerance and by listening to each other, and with empathy for the other's pain and distress. We must not patronize and be intolerant of our partner's feelings, since this will come back to us like a boomerang.

When conversing with each other, we must make sure to have steady eye contact. Gazing in each other's eyes expresses intimacy and openness. People who avoid looking at each other create an emotional block and put up an imaginary wall. Their partner will feel as though they are talking to a wall, as though their words are not being received earnestly by the other. They grant the relationship a technical, superficial and shallow character.

In order to make the relationship deeper and closer, it is recommended to speak about feelings, desires and grievances (also mutual grievances). A relationship devoid of emotional intimacy lacks a solid base, it is unsteady and unstable. It is based mostly on financial, familial, material and utilitarian interests, and the like. But this kind of relationship can easily break once any of these interests loses its significance.

The English poet John Dar said about love: "'Tis got by chance, 'Tis kept by art."

And poet Shaul Tchernichovsky commented on the importance of love in a relationship: "Where no love is, there is death."

\*\*\*

Let us always remember: it is the obligation of both partners, at every age and stage in their joint lives, to invest in their relationship: in a common interest, in being joyful, in experiences they can share. This will promise a life filled with happiness and openness.

# CHAPTER 62

# Leave the Nest!

**Nobody teaches us how to be parents, even though we are faced with incomparably complicated tasks that sometimes seem to contradict each other. Parents must teach their children to be independent, to adjust to a competitive and compassionate-less society, to be ambitious, to take responsibility, to have human values and rely on themselves alone, and yet at the same time, they must give them endless love, attention, and the feeling of safety and protection.**

Parents must maneuver in a very narrow space: between casting responsibility on their child and raising them to be independent and responsible, and between the natural inclination to shield and protect them from the harshness of lies, the evil and cruelty in the world.

*American author and educational speaker, Leo Buscaglia, said: "The only thing of value we can give kids is what we are, not what we have." (from the lecture "Love, Choice, Responsibility," available on YouTube)*

Most parents are wired with natural emotions that are meant to protect their children. We wish to save them from pain and lack and allow them to live their lives in a Utopian reality, one in which all their physical and emotional needs are met. However, together with our will to protect them, we must be careful not to castrate them. Over-protection might deny them the ability to function independently in society and build their lives. Over-protection might deny them the ability to build their lives independently, without depending on their parents. They may feel lack of confidence when their parents are physically absent, they may fear moving homes, traveling abroad, living abroad temporarily, going off to university – when their parents are not around.

Once our children have become adults, we must train ourselves to believe in them. To completely release our control. Our own lack of confidence and the anxiety that we feel about them might emanate outward and destabilize their belief in themselves. We must emanate to them, at all times, that they have the proper tools to handle this complex life, to succeed in their careers and build a happy family life. We must send them the message that we trust them—one hundred percent—to deal with the tasks in front of them, and that we are willing to support them logistically, financially, and emotionally should they need us to, according to our abilities and strength.

*Søren Kierkegaard, the Danish philosopher, said: "A son is like a mirror in which the father sees himself, and for the son in turn the father is like a mirror in which he sees himself in the time to come."*

Over-concern and desire to protect our children and fulfill their every need, prevents them from having to cope and they will not grow up to be responsible adults. The problem in this case will become ours, not theirs. Our bear hug might harm them and prevent them from real competition in life and the ability to spread their wings. We may find them depending on us even as adults.

*Janusz Korczak, the great physician, author and educator who was murdered with his students in the concentration camp Treblinka, said: "It is not enough to love children, we have to give them the same rights and rules that are binding for adults."*

\*\*\*

Let us release our children. Let them spread their wings and build their lives independently and according to their hearts' desires.

# CHAPTER 63

# To Compromise or Give up?

**There is no person who does not makes certain compromises in their life, but every person must live with awareness and understand what area in life they are compromising on and what is the price they are paying for it. The decision of the field and what to compromise on is subjective, and is made by every person according to their priorities.**

I'll give some examples: a couple lives in a small apartment, but prefers to travel abroad each year instead of buying a bigger apartment and paying off a mortgage for years. This decision, apparently, gives them energy, joy and experiences for a whole year. Obviously, they do not want a financial burden weighing on them every month, forcing them to lower their quality of life and binding them to a demanding workplace. Commitment to a mortgage or to other financial commitments minimizes our bargaining power. It is for this reason that we stay in a workplace that is less than satisfactory. We compromise on our professional satisfaction and quality of life in the workplace in order to gain a better quality of life and a better living environment for us and our family.

*Many people compromise on their relationships also, when they aspire to live with a sense of financial security and peace of mind, they pay the price of loss of intimacy in their relationship. A relationship protects the individual when two people carry the overall responsibility for the family.*

As sole providers they will have to lower their quality of life and handle the burden of life on their own: raising the children, caring for aging parents, illnesses, dealing with authorities, social life without a partner and so on and so forth. People who choose to leave their partners, choose to compromise on physical comfort, financial security, quality of life, occasionally complicated relationships with the children because of the separation, and receiving the status of "single," which will definitely separate them from some of their friends.

Our society is a familial society that encourages "coupling." Single and solitary people are forced to celebrate the holidays alone, unfortunately, and that is quite a heavy emotional burden.

When do people decide to pay this heavy price and dismantle their family? When they reach the conclusion that staying in the relationship is harmful to their soul and spirit. When they stay in a relationship that is not beneficial, and they pay for it with loneliness, depression, a constant feeling of emptiness, anger, anxieties, feeling a lack of vitality and passion. In this situation they choose to save their souls and leave their partners.

In which area is it best to compromise? Every person must decide according to their emotional needs and their priorities. There are those for whom the social status that is attained by a "successful" marriage, is more important than fulfilling their personal needs. There are those who are able to satiate their spirits even if they are in an unsuccessful relationship. They experience personal experiences on their own, like classes, workshops, trips abroad, friends, exercise, cultural activities and other pleasures that fill their spirits. However, it is important that we all know that in this situation, they are not treating their relationship problems, but running from them. They are building a reality of their own, in which they can live and function reasonably. They are not really in a relationship; they are giving up on emotional intimacy and living in a fictitious relationship.

I recently read that a large percentage of couples are actually living in this type of compromise. It is clear to them that the person they are living with will not change. They are trying to turn lemons into lemonade and make the most out of the relationship they are in. It is clear to everyone that this is a kind of compromise.

It is important to know that there is no one truth that is equal for all. Coupledom is a blend of two people with different emotional needs, coming from different families, living side by side under one roof, trying to create unity within their relationship and within their family. They must feel that they are both gaining from the relationship and benefiting from it. A situation in which one person is pleased but the other is miserable, needs questioning. It means the couple is not communicating with each other. People are supposed to know what their partner feels about the relationship. This is the first rule: openness.

\*\*\*

I do not suggest that anyone put up with violence in a relationship or emotional abuse. Absolutely not! This is a red line that must not be crossed. Beyond this, every person must decide how much they are willing to compromise. The only thing that determines this is the person's internal experiences.

# CHAPTER 64

# The Right to Always Be Secure

**The feeling of safety, physically and emotionally, is a basic and important feeling for a person and provides a healthy foundation for their sense of security, for realizing their human potential and for happiness.**

**Physical security***: literally means, physical and existential safety from dangers like violence, cold, hunger, illnesses, terror, weather damages and the like. Whoever has a roof over their head, an income and proper housing, and is free of violence and their life is not in danger—is a secure person.

**Emotional security***: This is a subjective feeling that accompanies a person throughout their life, and it determines their quality of life. In order to be a complete person who lives their life to the fullest, one must feel a deep feeling of security, be free of fear and threats to their life in and outside the home. They must feel a sense of security anyplace they stay. This feeling comes only from their internal experience, from their inner self, their "inner home," on a deep level of consciousness.

Psychiatrists have compared the human psyche to an iceberg. Most of the iceberg is hidden and goes deep down to the depths of the ocean. So too is a person's psyche—surfacing from deep within the subconscious. Oftentimes, the person does not understand the meaning or origins of their own emotions. Primary emotional experiences of a child or baby are burned on the psyche's "hard drive" while they are still in infancy, and more often than not, it is the initial experiences of the newborn that will shape the adult's view of reality, their life experiences and quality of life.

There are people on our planet that are day-in-and-day-out under real threat of survival. In many parts of the world, wars are being fought, natural disasters strike, hunger and calamities frequently threaten the locals. There are those who experience violence and humiliation in their home. They are robbed of their basic human right to live their lives with dignity, calmness, security, and being free of physical or verbal abuse.

Every child, whoever they are, is entitled to feel calm and safe, entitled to feel warmth, love, peace and have their physical and emotional needs met. A baby that feels lack in any of these areas will feel a void in their soul, and will spend their whole life trying to fill it. They will try and seek out the love and warmth they did not receive. Research done on orphans that did not receive warmth, hugs and physical closeness found that these babies were in a high risk group for developing diseases. In many cases, these babies died in their first few years as a result of emotional neglect.

*American statesman, Frederick Douglass said that "It is easier to build strong children than to repair broken men."*

A person who endured a lack of security as a child, an atmosphere of fear or violence and experienced a traumatic childhood in constant vigilance, adapted (or became attached) to living life with a constant sense of vigilance and readiness deep in their consciousness for any danger. They will have a hard time living a routine life, in peace and tranquility, as most people do, because this will seem not normal to them. The constant tension that they feel in their consciousness will accompany them throughout their daily lives, and they will need therapy and constant upkeep of their spirit in order to change their consciousness and practice a new consciousness of calmness and security. Taking responsibility and putting in the effort into their emotional state and consciousness will pay off greatly. Their lives will become much calmer and their quality of life will improve immeasurably.

Politician and businessman, Mitt Romney said: "Leadership is about taking responsibility, not making excuses."

*Or as Louise Hay said: "Thoughts create reality. Think positive thoughts about yourselves and your lives." (From YouTube video https://www. youtube.com/watch?v=8RPXgv67sms)*

Sometimes, a person who did not feel secure in their early years of childhood, will give up their emotional needs in order to connect with their most basic need for security. They will pay for this with anxiety, depression and repeated and recurring crises. Occasionally, they will give up on intimacy and happiness and settle for a life of emptiness, in order to feel the basic feeling of stability and security in life, but this will be nothing but an illusion of security.

A real sense of security comes from a person's inner power. Their mental and emotional forces will give them strength. This force comes from the universe, from God, from the cosmic energy that created them. A person who experienced a difficult childhood, who was able to survive it and build a life of meaning for themselves—is sure to have etched in their soul the truest priorities for life and the correct proportions. They will have ingrained in them a sense of joy, optimism and self-belief, and these will pave the path to happiness and internal peace.

\*\*\*

"Our greatest glory is not in never falling, but in rising every time we fall," said the great Chinese philosopher Confucius. Think about it.

# SECTION 11

## VALUES AND MORALS

# CHAPTER 65

# The Basis for Emotional Strength

**The most important strengths in life are a person's moral, ethical and mental strengths. Unfortunately, power gained by finances or status are quite often temporary and misrepresented. So is one's health. All the rest are external, insignificant and inconsequential façades in the larger context of a person's life and moral purpose.**

*Rabbi and poet of the Middle Ages, Yehuda Alharizi wrote: "The spirit yearns for morals like the earth yearns for the light."*

Optimistic people, with self-confidence and principles of social justice will always find a way to deal with financial, familial, personal and various other difficulties. Their strong belief in themselves, in human nature, in humanity and compassion, will help them handle difficult situations. Emotional strength is not necessarily something innate, but is instead learned through a process of education and personal growth.

Vagueness and instability in life are a bad situation in all respects. I am referring to lack of confidence in the workplace, fluctuations in one's personal life or lack of basic financial security. This pendulum leads to an emotional pendulum—and emotional vagueness is much worse than physical instability. Contrarily, a person who relies on a solid ethical foundation, who has clear moral priorities, focused goals, clear boundaries, and lack of vagueness—will be able to attain physical and emotional stability. They will feel easiness in their life, security, peace and calmness, and will also create a calm life in reality as well.

*Buddha said: "Peace comes from within. Do not seek it without."*

There are people who, for whatever reason—personal, familial, lack of emotional maturity—have blurry boundaries in their lives. They have not "decided" yet what is really important to them in life and what isn't. They have a hard time deciding where to invest their emotional energy, they lack a moral backbone and clear focus on their goals, and they are subject to, like a tent shaking in the wind, the pressures of their surroundings and external influences. These people, who have not yet crystallized a strong and solid worldview, are more vulnerable health-wise. Their bodies, which are fully dependent on their still disunited spirits, will not be strong enough to withstand the pressures of life. They lack the emotional and physical strength necessary for dealing with the challenges of life. They will also be vulnerable and sensitive to illnesses.

A strong, unified spirit, with a clear and strong moral stance, will support the body, and even if it does fall ill, it will have greater chances of easily recovering. On the other hand, a body that is subject to external influences and anchors, its unstable spirit swinging like a pendulum, a body that does not rely on a strong emotional and moral backbone—will have lesser chances of dealing with an illness. Emotional and spiritual strength protect a person's health as well.

A person who has a foundation of inner support and a solid foundation of inner control will rely on themselves and their loved ones. A strong foundation of inner support will guarantee a person's foundation of external support from family, friends and other people who love them. At times of crisis, God forbid, they will stand by their side. Contrary to them, a person who is spiritually weak, who lacks inner support, might find themselves without external support. People can sense who they can rely on, and it is likely they will not find many friends in their surroundings or at least not true friends. People are drawn to strong and stable people, not to people who are like a swinging pendulum. Our desire for stability causes us to connect with strong people who have solid backbones, who serve as our role models.

*Woodrow Wilson, 28th president of the United States, said: "The difference between a strong man and a weak one is that the former does not give up after a defeat."*

*Even Oprah Winfrey emphasizes the need of finding a purpose and calling in life, alongside the commitment to do our best in any area we work. (from "Oprah's 10 life lessons", available on YouTube https:// youtu.be/Zugaw67YXpw)*

*** 

I recommend that we all formulate a clear agenda for life. About our goals, aims, values, boundaries. I recommend that we set priorities and let people around us sense them. It isn't enough to say, "It's important to me to spend time with my children" or "It's important to me to invest in them," and simultaneously hardly ever see them.

Invest in the people you love. This is a long term investment that will always repay you in kind. Live up to the goals you set for yourself and lead your life according to their guiding light.

# CHAPTER 66

# Test Yourself: What is Your Value Scale?

**I suggest you test yourself from time to time: What are your most basic values? What will you never compromise on? Does the truth guide you? How often do you use lies and manipulations to achieve your goals? Are you loyal and honest? Do you stand behind your word? Can you look people in the eyes and look at yourself in the mirror?**

*German writer and poet, Johann Wolfgang von Goethe, wrote about this: "One cannot always be a hero, but one can always be a man."*

I ask these questions, because many people tend to sometimes forget these basic values, due to the pressures of life or other difficulties or circumstances.

It is important that we remember our system of values all the time, because that is our anchor for our lives. It is important that we mold for ourselves a solid and clear worldview which will clearly define our moral boundaries. Do not leave vague areas in your life. Act with transparency toward others and toward yourself. Do not make excuses to others and to yourself in order to justify bad behavior.

\*\*\*

Bottom line: Be honest with yourself and connect with your inner truth, and always act in accordance with your value system in all areas of life.

# CHAPTER 67

# What Are You Projecting?

**Let us try and imagine that we are in the center of a big balloon, while the circles of air around us are the people we come across in life.**

The circles closest to us are those people who surround us our whole lives. These are the people who are irrevocably connected to us, by choice or not by choice. By choice, of course, is our close family, our partner and friends. Around this is a larger circle of people we do not choose: extended family, work colleagues, classmates, neighbors, clients, people with whom we have professional relationships, and others. They are all in contact with us, but each one of them sees us from a different angle. Each one obviously encounters a different aspect of our personality. Nevertheless, our basic humanity is the same and manifests in all functions we fill in our lives. A person cannot change their character and essence. They carry with them to every place and every role their personality and character traits.

Try and define for yourself: What kind of atmosphere do you create in your "life balloon?" Is the atmosphere around you a calm, serene, warm and loving one? Does it emanate compassion, acceptance, tolerance, softness? Or does it emanate criticism, supervision, stubbornness, cynicism or aggression?

Does the humane and spiritual atmosphere that you create around you draw people toward you or vice versa? Do they feel confidence and fun in your company, or do they feel threatened and subject to criticism and judgment? Do you create a calm atmosphere or a stressful one? Do you strengthen the people around you and accept them with empathy, or do you hurt them, whether intentionally or not?

*Abraham Lincoln said about this: "To ease another's heartache is to forget one's own."*

*And Saint Augustine of Hippo, Christian philosopher and theologian and one of the Latin founders of the church, said: "We do not know another person, but through friendship."*

Do you see and feel the person in front of you? Are you sensitive to their presence and sensitivities? Are you willing to hear criticisms from them about yourself? Do you conduct a conversation with them? Do you speak with them or to them? Do you have the ability to listen to their personal story without immediately bringing an example from your life or your child's life?

The responses might answer some existential questions you carry within you.

An empathetic and accepting relationship with the people around you creates an environment of creativity, growth and development in a positive direction for your life and for the lives of those around you. It may assist you in any professional role you have, in any hobby and personal path you choose. The choice to make the people around you equal partners comes from the understanding that this is a "win-win" situation.

We have already stated that the choice to see all the people around you as completely equal, is a humane choice, but it is also a practical one. You can always turn them into partners and helpers in any matter you initiate and wish to promote. This is a wise and correct decision on an interpersonal level and in every other respect. Indeed, you will not succeed in every instance, but even the majority of cases will give you many points of merit and strong cards for life, something that will help you progress, in the present and the future.

***

Always be in the position of one who gives of themselves and their light to others. Poet and playwright William Shakespeare defined it accurately in the play "The Merchant of Venice:" *"How far that little candle throws his beams! So shines a good deed in a weary world."*

# CHAPTER 68

# Pass On Knowledge to Future Generations

**It is not only academia that plays an important role in attaining knowledge and education. It is the elder educated generation, the supreme specialists of their fields, who are obligated to the universal and human mandate: to pass on to future generations their full human and professional knowledge (and it does not matter if they work in the free professions, or if they are academics, artists, musicians, technical professionals and so on).**

*American politician, scientist and writer Benjamin Franklin said: "An investment in knowledge pays the best interest."*

*And Greek philosopher Epictetus said: "We must not believe the many, who say that only free people ought to be educated, but we should rather believe the philosophers who say that only the educated are free."*

Human research is all built from layers. Each study is built on top of that which preceded it and adds additional layers. All technological knowledge depends on being passed on to the next generations. This knowledge is never, under any circumstance, the private asset of one person or another.

Moreover, I believe that any person who holds professional knowledge, is bound by moral law to pass it on. It does not matter if the person in front of them is their official student or not. Even more so, they must take advantage of every opportunity to influence their colleagues based on their understandings.

"Academic selfishness" means closing oneself off in the ivory tower of academia. Academics who do not take advantage of the full breadth of their knowledge to make society a better place, are transgressing against their purpose.

Researchers and knowledge-holders must make their knowledge the property of the public and society in order to create a more tolerant and enlightened society. There is no value to the amount of books on the shelves of a library if the information is not used to make human society better, more just and moral.

***

We will finish with the words of Leonardo Da Vinci, of the great Renaissance artists: *The acquisition of any knowledge is always of use to the intellect, because it may thus drive out useless things and retain the good. For nothing can be loved or hated unless it is first known.*

# SECTION 12

## THE UNIVERSE, NATURE, AND US

# CHAPTER 69

# Spring, Summer, Autumn, Winter... Spring

**Not long ago, I watched a movie that enchanted me. The Korean film "Spring, Summer, Autumn, Winter... Spring" portrays the life of a monk living in solitude by a magical lake in Korea. The monk mentors a young boy in nature, and teaches him the meaning of life. The landscapes in the film are astonishing, the dialogues are few, but it seems they are not necessary. The images tell the story and convey the messages to us.**

While watching the film, I didn't fully understand its meaning. At night, I woke up and tried to reconstruct and understand the deeper meaning of the scenes. I did so with enthusiasm and excitement, like someone discovering a hidden secret.

The charm of the film is found in the educational process that the heroes go through with the monk. They learn some foundational principles of life: The first principle: the principle of simplicity and modesty, being satisfied with little. The monk's physical needs are few, and he gives respect to the universe and the entire animal kingdom, including the cat, the fish and even the snake. The message: all living creatures have the right to exist on this planet, although he does warn the boy to be wary of the snake.

The universe takes care of all living creatures on the planet. They all have a living space and can live harmoniously with each other. Man is part of the divine sphere, and so he naturally fits in with the cosmic existence. Everyone in the universe has a part. Man has no right to take the life of another living creature in nature, or to torture other animals. He teaches the boy a lesson he will never forget.

The monk teaches us something about love. It must not be possessive. Our beloved is not our possession. Immense passion leads to disaster. We must restrain ourselves, even with love, not to be possessive and obsessive and not hold on so tightly.

Another principle: Man's insignificance. A person must not be conceited over other humans, animals or their own power. They must know their place in the universe and the fact that they are transient and must restrain their ego.

The principles of serenity and self-restraint in man's ways are a common thread throughout the whole film. The film teaches us about the importance of routine and monotonous work. These are what give a person inner peace and balance. Life is made up of small moments of doing, and little events, not big occurrences.

The monk's love for others, his tolerance and peace, emanate onto his surroundings a sense of holiness, and serve as an inspiration for those around him.

# CHAPTER 70

# We Were All Made in His Image

**Every person is made in God's image. In every one of us is a cosmic element, a divine spark that gives us life and a compilation of qualities, feelings and abilities.**

**It is important that people who were blessed with talent, external beauty and other blessings, know that these are gifts from God, and that they feel no pride, vanity or superiority over others.** They did not work for these gifts and did not contribute to their development. They are not the source for the divine spark in them, but the vessel which contains material matter.

The source of the blessing is in the infinite universe. Modesty is an important trait. We must cherish the human skills we are blessed with and use them wisely to benefit mankind. All humans on the planet carry the responsibility to shine their light on those around them. To influence the world with their talents, hearts and emotions, and harness their qualities for the good of human society.

Every human is transient, every person has a purpose in life and they must fulfill it. If during life, a person has not contributed from their soul, spirit and talents to the universe and society—they have missed their calling.

*Rabbi Abraham Isaac Kook said: "If we forget our greatness, we forget ourselves." (from the book "Orot Hakodesh")*

Many people live their lives with the expectation that some external element will save them from their feelings of emptiness. Cause a change in their lives through some "miracle" or an external "heavenly event." There is no greater mistake. "Happiness is not a solution but a way of life" said a wise man, once. In the play "Waiting for Godot," Samuel Beckett shows us that God is in every person and every place.

*As Mother Teresa, nun, humanitarian activist, and Nobel Peace Prize winner, said: "We must know that we have been created for greater things, not just to be a number in the world, not just to go for diplomas and degrees, this work and that work. We have been created in order to love and to be loved."*

*And Galileo Galilei, Italian physicist, astronomer and philosopher, said: "You cannot teach a man anything; you can only help him find it within himself."*

\*\*\*

The keys to personal happiness are within each of us, and we must find these keys within ourselves. "Redemption" and happiness are in our hearts and souls, and to reveal them we must develop our consciousness. "Spiritual work" will enable us to remove the sand covering the inner well inside us and uncover the vitality and joy that exists in each and every one of us.

## CHAPTER 71

# The Strengths to which We Are Privileged

Every person has a divine spark inside them. In every person is a human element, an attribute, a value that differentiates them from other people. A person must recognize their prominent attribute, the one which sets them apart from other people and is considered their strong suit. They must enhance it and use it optimally in their life. This added value may help them in a time of trouble or crisis, and determine their fate in a situation of danger/emergency/threat, at a crossroads, when facing a loss of income, and so on.

And so, for example, a person who is blessed with the quality of optimism and joy of life must improve and enhance their optimistic character. They must enrich their life spiritually, learn and study, attend workshops and be in a constant process of spiritual development. They must turn these qualities into an anchor for them and for those around them. It is recommended that every person live life in a constant process of spiritual development.

*As Helen Keller, author and social activist who was deaf, blind and mute, said: "Optimism is the faith that leads to achievement. Nothing can be done without hope and confidence."*

Let us imagine for a moment that a person's workplace is undergoing organizational changes that entail the termination of certain positions. Our hero is also a candidate for termination. Assuming the other candidates all have the same professional and organizational skills and are experienced in their field, how will the superiors choose who to fire? It is likely that they will take into consideration the candidate's most prominent quality: joy of life and optimism, the ability to create a pleasant atmosphere, calmness and confidence, and the ability to strengthen their colleagues' spirits at times of crises and help them move forward. In the end, this quality will decide their fate, and thanks to it, they will not lose their source of income.

*Colin Powell, former US Secretary of State, stood for the importance of this quality when he said: "Perpetual optimism is a force multiplier."*

Another example: during the Holocaust, people's lives were saved thanks to their dominant qualities. For example: people with resourcefulness and courage, took chances and risked their lives. They initiated action that saved their lives. Other people survived during the Holocaust because they used the abilities and skills they were blessed with, such as their talents for music, boxing, sewing and so on. People who played in the horrible Auschwitz Orchestra survived thanks to their musical gifts. People who could dream a different reality for themselves, were those who survived in many cases.

*Jonas Salk, The Jewish-American scientist who developed the vaccine for Polio, said: "Hope lies in dreams, in imagination and in the courage of those who dare to make dreams into reality."*

And Dietrich Bonhoeffer, German theologian and Anti-Nazi dissident, said: "The essence of Optimism is that it enables a man to hold his head high, to claim the future for himself and not to abandon it to his enemy."

*\*\*\**

Identify the dominant quality in your character. Enhance it, improve it, and bring it to the level of an art-form; use it throughout your life. This will be your contribution to yourself, your environment and the universe.

# CHAPTER 72

# Go Outside!

**A sense of connection with nature may be a wonderful gift that can give us a sense of magical merging with the universe and emotional strength. Usually, a sense of calm and serenity follows. Some of us will feel this when standing by the blue ocean and listening to the sound of the crashing waves. Others may find the grace of creation in the desert and its wild landscapes.**

*Janusz Korczak, the great educator, demonstrated this well: "How wonderful it is that one can gaze for hours at a forest, at a single tree in it, at a single leaf on it, at a single vein on the leaf—and marvelous hours course and flow through the soul."*

The silence of the desert contains in it the Godly code. Out there, far away from the company of men, whilst listening to the deafening silence around us, we can truly listen to ourselves. I know quite a few people who, during times of stress and tension, when big decisions must be made in their personal or professional lives, go out to the desert. A short stay in the silence and solitude, even for twenty-four hours, might give us the proper perspective and help us choose the right path for ourselves.

The common phrase "clear my head" perfectly describes the process we go through when staying in the desert for a day or two, or when staying in greener pastures and listening to a cascading river. Most of us will return from there with a stronger opinion, optimism, peace of mind, and decisions that have ripened in us about our personal and professional future paths. The good energies will do their part and bring the subconscious into full consciousness regarding what is necessary and correct in our lives.

# CHAPTER 73

# Thank You For This Life

**Let's adopt a rule: To not take life for granted. Let's consider life to be the most wonderful gift we have ever received, cherish it every day, and never take it for granted.**

Confucius said: "Everything has beauty, but not everyone sees it." We must treat all assets in our life this way. We must not take for granted our freedom, our health, our relationship, our beloved family and everything we have in our lives, material, social, cultural and emotional achievements.

*Writer Charles Dickens said: "Reflect upon your present blessings—of which every man has many—not on your past misfortunes, of which all men have some."*

Cherish the most trivial of things:
For your morning yogurt—give thanks,
The view of the blossoming tree—cherish.
Be thankful for the smiles on your children's faces,
For your body that allow you to walk places,
To swim and enjoy intimacy with your partner.
Be thankful for a pleasurable vacation day,
As well as for a casual routine day.

This routine, which we take for granted—is something we miss dearly when things go wrong in life.

And to those who incessantly complain about their workplace, about the stress, paycheck, the boss, remember always that this job gives you an income and a respectable and decent life for you and your children. This job gives you pride and purpose and allows you to fulfill your abilities.

Do not whine about the small mishaps of life. Their weight is like that of a feather. They are gone with the wind and it's a shame to let them darken your mood. If you minimize them, you leave plenty of room for joy. Move them aside, and do not invest in them thought that eats up your mental and emotional energy.

Rabbi Nachman from Breslov's *approach emphasized the immense importance of feeling joyful: the simple joy, the kind of joy that is unconditional and does not depend on money, material things or external things. Its source is in the heart. This is joy of life.*

Steer clear of people who rob you of your energy. Seek those who infect you with their happiness, optimism, and positive outlook on life. Stick to those people and get inspired by them. Afterward, invent yourself each day anew. Build something unique of your own, and that something will attract people to you like a magnet.

Do not judge others. Always try and imagine that your soul is entering their bodies and living their lives. Imagine yourself in the other person's shoes. Try to feel their emotions and think their thoughts. Experience their experiences, understand their motives, wonder why they are angry, what is bothering them and what they are afraid of.

*Let's remember the words of Rabbi Nachman from Breslov: "It is better to fail at baseless love than at baseless hatred."*

\*\*\*

Teach yourself this technique of getting inside someone else's mind and body, and it will enable you to see the good in every person, and show them empathy, compassion, and love.

# CHAPTER 74

# And You Shall Choose Life

*The end, which is also the beginning*

**Choosing life** means not losing hope in spite of experiencing countless disappointments.

**Choosing life** means not losing faith in yourself and others.

**Choosing life** means understanding that you haven't yet used even a tenth of your abilities.

**Choosing life** means understanding that there are millions of opportunities in the world that you haven't yet seized.

**Choosing life** is understanding that at any moment you can turn in a thousand new directions.

**Choosing life** is understanding that you must thank God or the universe every day anew for what you have: for your health, for the people you love and who love you, and for the fact that you are even here right now.

**Choosing life** is being grateful for your workplace, even if it does not completely fulfill all of your aspirations. Recognize its advantages, and at the same time look for alternatives that will satisfy you emotionally.

**Choosing life** is understanding that the reality of your life is utterly subjective and depends on the glasses you wear. Pink, or God forbid, black. Your point of view is your life. Period.

**Choosing life** is filling yourself with energies each time anew and finding the way to do so.

**Choosing life** is understanding that the "breaking points" in your life are an inseparable part of life and they pass just as they came.

**Choosing life** means that you do not need external approval for your talents, amazing personality and your right to happiness.

**Choosing life** is understanding that internal happiness is the greatest treasure you can find and wish for yourself, and it is the result of an internal and personal decision.

**Choosing life** means that every moment must be seized, because the frenzy of time does not stand still.

**Choosing life** means making the most of the present, not suffering now so that the future can be better.

**Choosing life** means understanding that happiness does not depend on the material but the spiritual.

**Choosing life** means that you can give to others without detracting from yourself. The opposite. You will only feel fuller for it.

**Choosing life** means that you throw away everything you were told about dirty deals and stratagems. If you walk an honest path you will only see good, even if not right now. In the sum of all things, the gain is all yours.

**Choosing life** means loving yourself and those around you every day anew.

**Choosing life** is making peace with yourself and not trying to change. Also regarding others, accept them as they are, even if they are not perfect.

**Choosing life** is finding in the summer, in the winter, or in any time period, its little pleasures.

**Choosing life** is not being fearful, not even of yourself.

**Choosing life** means being honest with yourself and your surroundings. Of sounding your authentic voice.

**Choosing life** means no longer trying to convince others of your worth. It is enough that you know it.

**Choosing life** means goofing off from time to time.

**Choosing life** is understanding and recognizing the instances when your inner child is managing you, and you must hold them tight and protect them. Give them space in your feelings, but do not let them manage you.

**Choosing life** means understanding that your ego is only harming you and hurting your chances at success.

**Choosing life** means that nothing and no one can make you lose your enthusiasm.

**Choosing life** means not losing your innocence.

**Choosing life** means loving with full strength and power. Total love.

**Choosing life** means living with pleasure and fun and with full force.

Made in United States
North Haven, CT
25 June 2022